MW00788492

CHAPTER 18

Description

Corgis are one of the most famous smaller dog breeds, although technically they are medium-sized dogs. Closely related to Dachshunds, they are much sturdier and have a long history of being a hard-working dog. That means that they have much more energy than you may expect from such an apparently small dog, as well as an intellect that you really should not underestimate--especially when food is involved.

As its name suggests, the Welsh Corgi was a dog that was used to manage animals on farms in Wales. They had a wide range of tasks, from herding and leading to catching pests and keeping flocks of fowl in line. While they may not be as energetic as their larger counterparts, they are by no means sedentary dogs.

They may do as they are told, but only when it suits them. Corgis love their people unconditionally; however, that does not stop them from trying to have things their own way. They can be easily persuaded that you are alpha, but that does not mean that they will necessarily accept your rules. When left to their own devices, Corgis can figure out ways to do things that they know you will not approve of, and then try to hide the evidence. A Corgi can be both an incredibly mischievous and loveable dog that you will need to keep an eye on if you are to keep it out of trouble.

There are two types of Welsh Corgis: the Pembroke and the Cardigan. The Pembroke is the more popular and common of the two. Pembrokes are known for being incredibly friendly and affectionate with nearly everyone. Cardigans tend to be more reserved and quiet, and are more likely to be suspicious of strangers. However, one thing to keep in mind about Corgis is that all of them are unique individuals. You can encounter a Pembroke that is skittish and wary of strangers, or you may find a Cardigan that is every bit as outgoing and friendly as any Pembroke. Ultimately, each Corgi is an individual that is not defined by which type of Corgi it is.

Corgis are fantastic dogs and are easy to recognize with their long backs, short legs, and friendly expression. Their fox-like faces are topped with a couple of adorable ears that look as large as the Corgi's face.

With their long history and easy, friendly manners, Corgis are a great dog for most people. They make a great starter dog for those who have never had a dog, or a great challenge for those who want to be able to train their dog into something fascinating.

Introduction

Corgis are very loveable and intelligent little dogs that have the personality commonly associated with larger canines. They make great guard dogs and are excellent companions. With a physique that is unmistakably their own, it is easy to see why so many pet owners take their Corgis to so many different places. Perhaps the most famous Corgis are the ones that go nearly everywhere with the Queen of England; just another reason why the dogs are so popular and such a well-known breed.

These dogs were originally bred in Wales over the centuries to be excellent herding dogs, which accounts for their intelligence and sturdiness. It is also the reason why they are relatively easy to maintain – they are incredibly loyal and love being with their pack.

There are two types of Corgis: the popular and playful Pembroke and the dignified and companionable Cardigan. They have far more traits in common than differences, but the differences are enough that you can usually tell by looking at a Corgi which of the two types it is. However, their personalities are a little more distinct, so you should know which type is more likely to be the right companion for your lifestyle.

Regardless of which Corgi you choose, you have got a fantastic little friend who will be just as eager to try new things as you are.

Corgis are small and compact, and with their intelligence, they can actually get into many things that you don't want them to get into. Even a well-trained Corgi will get into mischief from time to time. You will learn to keep food out of their reach. It is also important to watch their caloric intake. This is somewhat easier to do than you may think as they have a relatively high energy level (although some Corgis are more sedate). While you can expel most of your Corgi's energy with a couple of long walks or a lot of indoor play, going for longer hikes will be beneficial because it will keep your canine in shape.

Corgis can be a lot of fun as long as you let them know you are the alpha dog. As long as you are consistent in training and care, your Corgi likely will be just fine with acknowledging that you are the head of the pack. That doesn't mean your canine won't try to get away with things, but that penchant for trouble is part of what makes Corgis so adorable and easy to love.

CHAPTER 1

Corgi Spotting Descriptions and Defining

Characteristics

There is very little chance of mis-identifying a Corgi once you have seen a couple of them. They are a short stout dog, similar to a Basset Hound, but with very distinctive ears (like radar dishes) and fox-like facial features.

They are small dogs, but they pack a very powerful personality and intellect into that small frame. Corgis are very clever and they are not afraid to let you know it. They are incredible companions that are easy to take on the road since they don't require much space.

*Photo Courtesy of
Kandace Wilkens*

Pembroke or Cardigan?

A Corgi looks like a Corgi, regardless of whether it is the very popular Pembroke Welsh Corgi or the more refined Cardigan Welsh Corgi. They have far more physical characteristics in common than they have differences, but you can still usually tell which type a Corgi is based on the color and a few other traits.

Appearance

Despite its short stature, the Corgi is considered to be a medium-sized dog because it is very stout and rather long in body. They are usually between 10 and 12 inches in height and weigh between 20 and 40 pounds. When you look at their heads and bodies, it appears that their legs simply did not grow in proportion to the rest of them. They have beautiful coats that come in several different colors:

- Black
- Tan and black
- Brindle
- Gray
- Mottled blue
- Red

Apart from their size and coats, the Corgis have two very distinguishable features – large, upright ears, and a fox-like face. Their ears are usually perked up, and Corgis hear exceptionally well with those ears (it is one of the reasons why they are notorious barkers). Corgi puppies look like they are made almost entirely of ears.

The fox-like face appears to have a perpetual smile, which is one reason why Corgis are such a popular dog – they both look and act happy most of the time.

Temperament

Pembrokes and Cardigans have more differences between their personalities than their physiques. However, some traits are fairly universal.

They are incredibly intelligent, and so as long as you are consistent and dedicated in your training regimen, you should have a fantastic companion. It is one of the reasons why they are so popular and why even those who have never owned a dog can enjoy them. Corgis quickly pick up on what you want during their training, although this does mean they also can figure out how to break the rules. If you aren't careful, you could end up being trained by your Corgi.

One of the few things they have in common with other small and medium-sized dogs is that they bark. A lot. This is one of the biggest complaints about Corgis. With their large sensitive ears, they hear virtually everything, and are very quick to alert everyone about what they hear. This is one of the main reasons that it is so important for you to socialize your Corgi – it keeps your canine from being disturbed by every little sound.

They are high-energy dogs, which means taking them on at least a couple of walks a day is the best way to ensure your Corgi does not cause a lot of problems.

They are working dogs, which means that there are several traits that you have to watch for, such as nipping. They make a great family dog, although they are not terribly fond of young children. The loud noises small kids make can be a source of pain and annoyance to them.

Like other intelligent working dogs, they tend to be individualistic and strong-willed. While this is a great trait for herding dogs, it is something you want to train them to avoid as a pet.

Finally, they may be individualistic, but they do not like to be alone for long. If they are left home alone over the span of a full eight-to-ten hour work day, they tend to get restless and anxious, which they act out on by destroying things. By training them you can easily fix these issues, but it is best that you not leave them alone for long stretches of time. If nothing else, having another dog around will help to soothe your Corgi.

It's a Pembroke!

While the two types look incredibly similar, you can tell if you are looking at a Pembroke Welsh Corgi by checking out a few different features.

Examining the Ears

The Pembroke's ears are more triangular so that the tips appear to be pointed. This actually emphasizes how pointed the Corgi face is, and looks particularly adorable when they are about to get a treat.

Observing the Tail

The Pembroke tail is also usually short to almost hidden. If you see a Corgi that appears to have virtually no tail, you are looking at a Pembroke Welsh Corgi.

Common Coats

While the coats tend to be less of an indicator than the other two features, Pembrokes usually have tan in their coats. You do find some that are mostly black and white, but if you look closely, there is usually some tan, at least on the face.

Height

Pembrokes tend to be shorter, although this won't help you much if you don't have one of each to check the height. Typically, you will need to rely on the other physical attributes to be able to identify which of the two kinds of Welsh Corgis you are seeing.

Temperament

The Pembroke is known for being the friendlier of the two (they are Queen Elizabeth II's favorite dog) and it is highly adaptable. When faced with a challenge, a Pembroke is more likely to change to match the environment. They also have a noticeably higher energy level than their

Photo Courtesy of Cassie Thwaites

counterpart, making them a better choice if you want a constant companion for outside excursions.

Their charming personality is what makes them the more popular of the two types as well. For those who want a constant companion without having to worry about the pup getting tired as quickly, this is the Corgi for you.

It's a Cardigan!

You can call the Cardigan Welsh Corgi the more dignified of the two types. They tend to be calmer, quieter, and a little less fond of changes. However, they have the more classic looking radar-dish ears that people associate with the Corgi. They may not be as popular as their close relatives, but they are still incredibly sweet.

Examining the Ears

Cardigans have ears that are much more rounded, giving them the appearance of having two large radar dishes atop their heads. The ears tend to be longer and are more obvious when the dog swivels them to hear everything going on around it.

Photo Courtesy of
Michele Eathorne

Observing the Tail

If you see a Corgi with a tail that appears to be of normal length, it is almost certainly a Cardigan. The long, wagging tail of a Cardigan is one of the two most distinguishable traits.

Common Coats

While you will need to focus on the ears and tail, you can make your first assessment by checking out the coat. The Cardigan tends to be the more colorful of the two types, with some having no tan or beige on them at all. If the Corgi's coat is mottled or brindle, it is almost certainly a Cardigan. If the coat is black and white, it is also probably a Cardigan, but you should check for tan and beige in the face--it could just be well hidden. There are also Cardigans that have the same coat coloring as Pembrokes, though, so it is just a way to make your initial guess as to the Corgi type.

Height

The Cardigan tends to be the taller of the two dogs, which is a moot point if you don't have both a Pembroke and a Cardigan nearby.

Temperament

Cardigans are the more relaxed Corgi and they prefer that things remain the same. They can adapt; they just are more likely to enjoy a routine that does not involve strangers. They are more likely to be alright with missing the occasional walk (they are less likely to have excess energy that they will need to take out on your furniture when you do miss walks).

A Quick Word on Temperament

While it is true that you can generalize the personality types based on the Corgi, every Corgi is different. You can find that your Cardigan is as adventurous and friendly as a Pembroke, or you may have a Pembroke that prefers a nice, quiet evening at home. Much of their personality has to do with their training and genetics. It certainly isn't a bad thing because all of the most basic personality traits are pretty universal, which is what makes the Corgi so popular in the first place – many people aren't even aware that there are two different kinds.

CHAPTER 2

Breed History and Characteristics

The birthplace of the dog is right there in its name – the Welsh Corgi. Originating in Wales, this dog was ideal for cattle herding in the cold, wet, rolling hills. Its compact size gave it a distinct advantage in looking after the herd as well, since it was much more difficult to kick than a larger dog.

Corgis have been around for centuries, perhaps millennia – long enough to have a legend about their origins.

Agrarian Wales and Herding Cattle

Neither the arrival and evolution nor the source of the name of the breed is known with any level of certainty. Both have been lost to history, making both the evolution and name a source of debate among Corgi and canine lovers. While the stories are a little tamer than the legends, there are still a lot of points that are up for debate, making the Corgi's history a rich tapestry of guesswork.

In the Early Days

First, we will take a look at the potential arrival of the dogs in Wales.

It is possible that either the Vikings or Celts brought an early version of the Corgi to the island. If the Vikings were the original source, the Corgi would have arrived some time during the 800s. If the Celts were the original source, they would have brought the dogs during the 1200s. There is not enough evidence to support either of these groups as the original source.

What is known is that the dogs were found primarily in Wales (which is why the source was either the Vikings or the Celts). They had a very clear purpose as well – they were an ideal cattle dog and guard dog, though initially they were only used at the front of a herd to ensure that predators were kept away from the cattle and flocks. Later, the people of Wales realized that the dogs were equally useful in driving the cattle, so the dogs were employed to protect and herd. This is where the Corgi's tendencies to bark often and nip came from, and those tendencies are still relatively strong today (although they can be managed with proper training). It is believed that at this point the original dogs were bred with sheep dogs to improve their herding instincts. This proved to be particularly useful for getting the cattle to market.

Cattle were not the only animals that Corgis managed. They also were responsible for the safety of domesticated flocks of fowl, a far less arduous task than herding cattle. Still, after protecting the flock from predators, the dogs had their hands full rounding up the birds for housing when dusk arrived. This is actually rather surprising if you know how much Corgis bark, but at the time, not all of them were so proficiently vocal. This was essential as birds tended to be nervous by nature, and barking would have scattered the birds instead of collecting them into a designated area. If you have ever tried to get fowl to move to a certain area, you can understand just how the Corgi got such a strong will.

Photo Courtesy of
Cassie Thwaites

Since they were small, Corgis were also an ideal dog for getting rid of vermin and pests. Over time, they were also employed to help with hunting since they could easily get into areas that were too small for larger, taller dogs.

They have always been an incredibly versatile and adaptable dog, which is a significant reason why they are so intelligent today.

It's All in the Name

There several theories about the origins of the Corgi name.

- It could have been the Celtic word for dog, considering there were not many breeds on the island.

- It could be a combination of two Celtic words, cor (dwarf) and ci (dog). Ci would have to have evolved to gi at some point, but that is how languages tend to work, so the explanation makes sense on a linguistic level.

- The word could have English roots and mean cur or dog. English words used to be pluralized with en or n, so the use of the word Corgwn could be a plural form of Corgi. This theory is supported by the number of 14th and 15th century songs that praise the Corgwn. At the time, cur did not have the negative connotation it has today – it simply meant a working dog (as opposed to a pet or upper-class dog).

All of these are very sensible and logical roots for the name of the dog. However, the most interesting tale comes from the legends around the breed.

The Corgi Legend

One of the theories behind the name Corgi actually ties into the legend. The dogs were said to be the companions of elves and fairies, doing the same work that horses did for humans. It was thought that Corgis would sneak away from their homes at night to be with their magical friends. They say when you look at Pembroke Corgis, the markings on many of them (white around their shoulders and neck) appear similar to little saddles, indicating their use as steeds by small creatures.

It is a very cute and enchanting legend for such a small dog packed so full of personality.

Tales of the Divergence of the Two Breeds

Cardigans are the older breed, with the beginnings of their existence being estimated at around 3,000 years ago. Of course, the breed was nothing like the Corgi of today (the current version was bred from the original dogs). They come from the same canine family that produced a similar looking long dog – the Dachshund.

It is believed that the current version of the Cardigan was bred from the dogs the Celtic tribes brought when they arrived in Wales.

The Pembroke Welsh Corgi is both better known and more popular than the Cardigan. The earliest records of the Pembroke date back to 1107, but little more is known about the early days of the dog. Some believe that they were the result of breeding with the Swedish cattle dog popular with Vikings. Others think that they are a mix of the original Corgi and the Spitz, a breed brought to Wales by Flemish immigrants.

The breed was not recognized until the 1920s, when the two types were lumped together as Corgis.

Photo Courtesy of
MaryAnn Carney

Quick Guide to their Best and Worst Traits

There is a lot to love about these dogs, and they are a great fit for many homes. However, they are not for everyone. They can make a great first dog if you have never had a dog before, but you should be aware of some of the traits that people find frustrating. If nothing else, you can prepare and train to minimize the aspects that you think are likely to bother you.

Best traits

Corgis are intelligent, fun-loving, and incredibly loyal. They love the people who are part of their pack and they get enthusiastic about going outside. They are known for being very dependable and easy to train, two things that make them fantastic for people who have not had a dog before.

Their small stature makes it easy to adopt and keep them active even in an apartment (although their tendency to bark may make them less than ideal for apartment living).

Photo Courtesy of
Caitlin Cassity

They have a big-dog personality. In other words, they love to learn new things, do tricks, and generally be active. Nor are they discouraged by the fact that they cannot keep up with larger dogs since they persist until they achieve their goals. Their personality is easily attributable to their history of being a working dog – they were treated like the bigger dogs, so they learned the same behaviors.

They love to be with people (sometimes a little too much) and will make you feel quite welcome when you get home.

Grooming is very easy because they have a short fur that does not mat easily .

Worst Traits

Easily the two most bothersome traits of the Corgi are its eagerness to bark and tendency to nip. You can train the nipping out of your young Corgi, but barking is something that many Corgis never overcome. It makes them great guard dogs as their voice is not that of a small dog, but it can quickly become a source of annoyance if you were not expecting such a vocal dog.

They have a tendency to eat more than they should (like many dogs), but with their small size this is a definite problem if you do not carefully monitor their caloric intake. With their long backs, Corgis need to maintain a healthy weight, something they struggle with because they love food. With their intelligence, they have been known to figure out ways of climbing up on chairs (after moving them) to reach food on tables and counter tops.

Both types of Corgis are prolific shedders. With their thick, short fur, they basically shed year round. Frequent grooming can minimize this, but you really cannot totally eliminate it.

They are full of energy, which is a great thing if you are an active person. If you do not like to go out regularly, or if you cannot go out almost daily, Corgis likely are not a great choice as a companion because they tend to be destructive when home alone for too long or when they do not get regular exercise.

They also tend to be stubborn and independent, which can be problematic if you are not assertive and consistent in your care of them.

A Royal Choice

One of the things that is almost always brought up when people discuss Corgis is that they are the choice canine of the Queen of England. All of her dogs are Pembroke Welsh Corgis.

Her love of the Corgis has seen her companioned with more than thirty Corgis over the course of her entire life. She received her first Corgi from her father, King George VI, back in 1933.

Interestingly enough, people actually use Corgis to try to predict the next name of members of the royal family. There is a game (and you can gamble if you think you can guess the next name correctly) where Corgis are given vests with the most likely name that will be given to the next member of the royal family.

Photo Courtesy of Cassie Thwaites

CHAPTER 3

The Ideal Home

Because of their size, Corgis can be comfortable and happy in most types of homes, including apartments (although your neighbors may not be happy with all of the barking). Still, there are some types of environments and lifestyles that are better than others.

Keep in mind that they are active dogs. It may not be required to have a large yard, but daily exercise is necessary. Corgis are also intelligent, which means you are going to need to dog proof certain areas of your home. Their ability to sneak food and their high energy level make regular activity a high priority. If you don't have a yard or enough room to really play in your home, you will need to live close to some place that you can take your Corgi to regularly. This could be a park or just a lot of sidewalks so that your Corgi gets a new walk with some regularity.

*Photo Courtesy of
Betsy Ellsworth*

Best Environment

Corgis are incredibly popular because of their size and amazing personalities. Because of the ease with which they can be trained, many people think they are the perfect dog to have. That may be true for many people, but like every other dog, there are optimal situations for them.

A Compact Canine for Any Home

One of the things that people love most about Corgis is their adorable little bodies. They look very similar to Dachshunds with their long bodies low to the ground, but they are much sturdier and wider than Dachshunds. Their weight qualifies them as medium-sized dogs, which can seem strange until you pick one up. Still, they don't even come up very high on an adult's shins. Their small stature and sturdy build means that they can easily sit with you on the couch or lie at the foot of your bed without taking up much space, yet there is more than enough dog to hug.

Photo Courtesy of
Tammie Songer

They don't require a large crate, either for travel or home use. Many Corgis have no fear and are excited about different adventures. Their presence can be very calming after a long day, and their enthusiasm can be contagious. Since they are able to go nearly everywhere you go without taking up much additional space, it is easy to see why people love owning them.

Even No yard is Fine – as Long as Your Corgi Gets Moderate Exercise

Photo Courtesy of
Betsy Ellsworth

It is nearly impossible to overemphasize the importance of exercise for Corgis. Keeping in mind their history as a highly adaptable working dog (herding, protecting, catching pests, hunting, and tending fowl), it should not come as a surprise that they have a lot of energy crammed into that small frame. You don't need a yard but you do have to be dedicated to taking them out for at least a couple of walks every day. Walking for the Corgi is more about moving around than it is about a bathroom break.

If you cannot take your canine out often, you need to have a yard where it can play and expend energy.

Exercise is essential for Corgis for two reasons: they gain weight easily and they may get destructive if they have pent-up energy. If you don't ensure that your Corgi has a way to get plenty of exercise, you really can't blame your dog for destroying anything within reach – and with such a sharp mind, they can get into places you would never think they could reach.

The bottom line is that a yard is not necessary as long as you have places where you can exercise nearby.

A Warning about Apartments and Barking

Those ears do exactly what you think they should do – they allow Corgis to hear things that even many other dogs don't notice. With such sensitive hearing, it should not be a surprise that these dogs are incredibly vocal. They will bark at pretty much anything, inside or outside of your home.

If their size makes them ideal for an apartment, their tendency to bark adds a caveat to that ideal. You either need to have walls that are thicker than those of the average apartment, you need to have neighbors who don't mind constant barking, or you need to train your dog to bark only at certain types of sounds. The third option is probably the most difficult to achieve as it means fighting centuries of developed instinct.

When you use the right tools or adopt a puppy from parents who are less likely to bark, you stand a better chance of training your Corgi to be quieter. After all, they are the same dogs that helped to manage flocks, which they couldn't do well if they barked incessantly. Just know that you may be taking on a Herculean task, and you will need to adjust accordingly. Also, plan for how to handle frequent barking since this will ensure that you can react quickly during training.

Floor Surfaces

Photo Courtesy of Sunny Hanford

The Corgi looks sturdy, but being so low to the ground does not mean that it is any easier for them to stop themselves on slick floors, such as hardwood or vinyl. Since they tend to get excited about playing, this often means they end up sliding into things. They will usually shake it off, but in the long run, this is not good for your Corgi.

You can either put down carpeting or nonskid throw rugs in the areas where your Corgi plays to help ensure that your canine stays safe.

Not Great with Young Children

There is a lot to love about Corgis, but one of the few concerns is that there are a relatively large number of them that are not fond of small children. Toddlers and other little people are roughly at the same height as a Corgi and that can create problems. Young children simply are not gentle, and Corgis do not like to be handled in a rough manner (they are used to being the herders, not the herded).

When you couple this with the fact that Corgis have incredibly sensitive hearing, you really cannot expect the dog to be fond of toddlers and other young people. This age group is also exploring the sounds they can make, and volume is not something they understand yet. When a young child starts screaming and crying, this can be physically painful for a Corgi. This means they can be less tolerant of (and less than pleased with) young children.

Ideal Lifestyle

First and foremost, Corgis want to be with you. Most of them hate to be alone, so if you have a Corgi, it is going to stay by your side as much as possible. That does mean that you need to be home more often than you are not at home, or you need to be able to take your dog with you when you are going to be gone for long stretches of the day.

They do need a lot of exercise, although not as much as many of the other working dogs since they are smaller. That doesn't mean that you can become complacent and skip walks, though. You really should enjoy being outside, and a Corgi can make your excursions that much more enjoyable.

Photo Courtesy of Liza Gagne

Strengths

One of the things that people love about Corgis is that they are incredibly attentive. They want to be with you, listen to you, and play with you. Of course, they also want to make the rules, but you can teach them that they are not the alpha dog so that they will listen better.

Corgis are also playful dogs and they are often described as being cheerful. Because of their size, it is easier to tire them out faster, although some have been known to only need a short break before being ready for more activity. They have a lot of spirit and love to be active, so the potential for games and other entertainment is nearly limitless.

Common Exercise Benefits

Another thing that is great about Corgis is that they can force you to exercise more without it feeling like a chore. However, you don't really have to do anything elaborate to keep them happily active. Unlike larger working dogs, Corgis are content with frequent walks, some yard play, and romping in the park.

By exercising with your Corgi, both of you are getting healthier and staying healthier. Your pup will be tired (at least for a few minutes) and you will have done something for yourself that you may not have done without your dog.

Exercise also keeps your Corgi entertained. Because they are intelligent dogs, they do not do well when they are penned up at home for days at a time. Nor do you have to exercise on a set schedule. When you and your canine go out to exercise on a regular basis, your Corgi will be happier.

A rousing game of fetch can be enough for Corgis to get some of that excess energy out. With their short little legs, they do not have to go as far to get adequate exercise. It doesn't mean you should skimp, though. If your Corgi plays fetch for twenty minutes straight and is still pretty excited, going for a walk will ensure that that energy is worn down before returning indoors.

Finally, because they are small working dogs, they love food but can gain weight quickly if not exercised often. Frequent trips outside will keep them mentally and physically healthy.

Beware of Loneliness and Boredom

Working dogs are notorious for shredding, tearing, and destroying anything within their reach when they are left alone without anything to do for long periods of time. Corgis are no different. In fact, they can

Photo Courtesy of
Jae Ojala

get anxious when left alone for long periods of time, significantly increasing the odds that you are going to come home to a complete mess in your home.

Corgis do not like to be alone. This is why many Corgis have at least one other canine companion. The second dog doesn't replace you, but it can make the Corgi feel a little more secure when you are not around.

The fact that they are intelligent can also be a problem because they can figure out how to do things that you would never imagine. For example, they can figure out how to move a chair away from the table so that they can hop up on the chair and then the table and eat anything you left on the table. Problem solving is something they do extremely well, and when they get bored or lonely, that can be dangerous, for them and for your home.

Shedding – The Two Shedding Seasons

Corgi coats are incredibly easy to manage, but those thick coats also shed in a way you would not believe. You can think of Corgis as having two shedding seasons– the first half of the year and the second half of the year. It is nearly mind blowing just how much dog hair these compact little canines can shed. Within a day or two, you will start to see little hair balls rolling around on the floor, and it will be practically impossible to ever completely get rid of them.

Frequent brushing will help, but you will still have dog hair all over everything in your home and your wardrobe. It is a relatively small price to pay for such an adorable and adoring dog, though.

Extremely Sensitive – They Hear Everything

Those large ears give the Corgi a sense of hearing that most animals lack, and it comes with two drawbacks: they are bothered by loud noises and they respond to virtually anything.

You must be careful around Corgis to make sure you do not hurt their ears. They are not bothered by their own barking, but loud noises and screaming can negatively affect them. It is why they tend to be wary or keep their distance from young children. Little kids tend to shriek and shout, and that can hurt the Corgi's ears. Loud noises are louder to your Corgi too, so you have to be careful of hurting them by taking them places where there is a lot of loud noise. It isn't so serious that you have to adjust your life around it, but it is something you should be mindful of for your Corgi's sake.

Their incredible hearing is why these dogs are notorious barkers. Any little sound can set them off. The odds are very high that you are going to have to learn to put up with a certain amount of unnecessary barking at what you think is nothing. They hear sounds you don't hear, and they are not afraid to speak up when they do.

A Little Dog for Those Who Love Big Dogs

If you love big dogs but do not have the space in your home for one, Corgis are a perfect alternative. They will give you the same kind of attention and affection that you would get from a Labrador or Golden Retriever without the size. They will be just as active and will help you feel better at the end of a long day. In the end, they just want to be with their people, playing and enjoying the outdoors.

Pembroke – Fun loving and Affectionate

Pembrokes are the more popular of the two Corgi types because they are more affable and affectionate. They want to be outside doing things and enjoying whatever you are doing. Your Pembroke comes from a long line of dogs known for herding and corralling much larger (and some smaller) animals. This makes your dog fearless and curious, which is a different kind of entertainment for you. They enjoy changes and can quickly adapt to new games and events.

Cardigan – Protective and Intelligent

Cardigans are the more sedate and relaxed of the two dogs. They are less likely to mind being home more (although they still require a good bit of exercise, so don't get too complacent). They prefer for things to be on a little more regular schedule, but they do still need activities to keep them mentally stimulated. They are more likely to be very protective of you (beyond just barking) and they tend to be more analytical than their Pembroke counterparts are. This means you need to be prepared to outsmart them if you are going to leave them alone or want to play a different game.

*Photo Courtesy of
MaryAnn Carney*

CHAPTER 4

Finding Your Welsh Corgi

If you have made it this far, you probably are excited about finding your own Corgi to take on adventures and relax with. Welcome to a whole new world of fun, entertainment, and love! Your decision is very likely to help you find one of the best friends you will ever have.

You have the foundations you need to understand what you are getting into. Now it is time to learn how you should go about finding your newest family member.

Your first two decisions will be the hardest:

- Will a Pembroke or a Cardigan be the right fit for your home?
- Do you want a puppy or an older dog?

Photo Courtesy of
Cindy Duwe

These are both tough questions. Each Corgi is different, so expecting your Pembroke or Cardigan to be exactly as they are usually stated to be probably isn't going to work. The information about their typical personalities is a guide, not an absolute. Ultimately, the answer depends on the second question – deciding on the dog's age when you get it. It's an even tougher question because one involves a lot more work while the other involves understanding the established personality of your pup.

Deciding Between the Pembroke and the Cardigan – Initial Considerations

Your first decision should be to select the type of Welsh Corgi you want – the Pembroke or the Cardigan. Your personality and lifestyle is very likely to line up with the personality of one or the other type better.

- Pembrokes are fun loving and adaptable. If you are constantly on the go and want to have a companion who will enjoy it, the Pembroke is a better choice for your lifestyle. While they do bark a lot, they are very friendly. They are a nearly perfect companion dog for active people.

- Cardigans like to move around, but they also know how to appreciate a relaxing evening at home. They don't require as much activity and they are better watch dogs since they are more protective. If you are looking for a dog that can enjoy the evening at home with you and is a better guardian, the Cardigan is a better choice.

Keep in mind that Corgis are all very individualistic, and just because you were looking for a particular personality does not mean you will get it. Much of your dog's personality will depend on how well you train your dog (if you get a puppy). If you choose an older dog, its personality is already established and the people taking care of the dog will be better able to tell you if the dog exhibits the kind of personality you want. Breeding makes their personality more predictable, but it is never guaranteed.

Adopting from a Breeder

Once you know which type is more likely to fit into your home best and you have decided you are prepared to dedicate a lot of time to training a puppy, it is time to start finding the breeder who is most likely to give you a healthy, happy Corgi puppy. You do need to be careful because there are many Corgi breeders out there. You want a breeder who cares as much (or more) about the puppies as about profiting from the sale. This means taking a good bit of time to thoroughly research breeders.

Finding a Breeder

Photo Courtesy of
Gayla Miller

You want a breeder who takes the care of the puppies seriously and shows them the necessary attention and care so that the puppies are well adjusted by the time they are ready to leave their mother. To begin, you need to research breeders and look at only the ones who show and title their dogs from the start. Odds are very good that you will end up on a waiting list, but it means that your puppy will be both mentally and physically healthy.

Once you have narrowed down the list of the breeders you will contact, you will need to call them and ask questions. Be prepared for this to take up to an hour per breeder (it may not, but it is best to plan on it) so that you can fully understand how much the breeder understands about the dog and how well the breeder takes care of the puppies.

- Ask them about the particular type of Corgi to find out if the breeder only focuses on the positives. A good breeder will want to make sure that you understand the potential problems of having a Corgi and will try to dissuade you if the negative aspects could be a problem for you.

- Ask about health tests and certifications. These points are covered in more detail in the next section, but your breeder needs to have all of the tests and certifications to ensure that you receive the healthiest puppy possible. Good breeders will often have guarantees against the worst genetic issues.

- Verify that the breeder will take care of all of the initial health issues, such as vaccines and worming. Puppies need to have these procedures started by the time they are six weeks old, which is well ahead of when the puppy can leave the mother. Vaccinations and worming occur every three weeks, so your puppy should be well into its initial health care (or even completely through the beginning phases) before it gets to your home.

- Find out if the breeder requires the puppy to be spayed or neutered when it reaches maturity. Many breeders require that the puppies be spayed or neutered as part of the contract. This is meant to be in the puppy's best interests.

- Ask if the breeder is part of a Corgi club or organization. Corgis have been around long enough that there are a number of codes and standards required of members who breed their Corgis. If you find a breeder who is part of a Corgi organization and cannot meet your request, that breeder can probably point you to a few other good breeders. The puppies from these types of breeders are much more likely to be healthy and happy as the breeders must be both conscientious and honest about the parents and the puppies.

- Find out what happens during the first phase of the puppies' life, and how the breeder takes care of the puppies during the earliest stage of their lives. This will help you know how much work you have to do as well. You will want to train your dog consistently, and that will be much easier if you continue what the breeder started. The breeder may also have begun different types of training, such as house and crate training. You will need to know that before getting your puppy home.

- Ask for advice on raising a Corgi. A good breeder can make recommendations and will give you options on how to handle some of the less enjoyable phases, as well as things that your puppy is likely to love. A great breeder will also be there to answer questions about your Corgi long after your dog has reached maturity. They are interested in the dog's well-being and are willing to answer questions over the Corgi's entire life span.

Health Tests and Certifications

For a dog with such a lengthy history, Corgis are incredibly healthy and relatively free of major genetic health problems. However, there are a few tests and certifications that should be conducted.

As the younger of the two types, Pembrokes do not require as much testing and certification:

- Hip dysplasia evaluations (OFA evaluation or a PennHIP evaluation)

- Eye examination by someone who is a member of the ACVO Ophthalmologist (they should be registered with either the OFA or the CERF)

Cardigans need a little more attention in terms of testing:

- Hip dysplasia evaluations (OFA evaluation, OVC, or a PennHIP evaluation)
- Eye examination by someone who is a member of the ACVO Ophthalmologist (they should be registered with either the OFA or the CERF)
- A DNA test for Progressive Retinal Atrophy (PRA)

There are no strict certifications, but you do want your breeder to be a part of an established club or organization.

- Pembroke breeders are usually part of the Pembroke Welsh Corgi Club of America, Inc., and they adhere to all of the regulations about breeding Pembroke Welsh Corgis. They also recommend that breeders provide a copy of the Code of Ethics for raising and having a Pembroke.
- Cardigan breeders can join the Cardigan Welsh Corgi Club of America, and they must adhere to specific guidelines.

Being a member of these organizations means that the breeders are obligated to meet a minimum set of requirements. If they do not meet these requirements, the breeders are not allowed to be members of the organizations. This ensures that breeders that belong to these organizations are reliable and predictable in the way they treat their puppies.

Contracts and Guarantees

Since these are dogs with a long history, it should not be a surprise that many breeders have contracts that you must sign before they will consider selling you a puppy. Many of them also have guarantees, which may or may not make you feel more at ease.

The guarantees state what the breeder is guaranteeing with your new dog. This usually includes information on the dog's health and recommendations on what the pet owner's next steps are. For example, it may recommend that you take your puppy to the vet within two days of arriving at home to ensure that the dog is as healthy as it is believed to be. In the event that a major health concern is found, the puppy will need to be returned to the breeder. It will also explain what is not guaranteed. The guarantee tends to be very long (sometimes longer than the contract), and you should read it well before you sign the contract.

In addition to the price of getting your dog, Corgi contracts ensure certain behavior by the new Corgi human parent. Corgi contracts usually come with a requirement to have the dog spayed or neutered once the dog reaches maturity (typically six months). The contract may also contain naming requirements, health details, and a stipulation for what will happen if you can no longer take care of the canine (the dog usually goes back to the breeder). They also include information on what will happen if you are negligent or abusive.

Puppy Genetics – the Parents

Because the breed has such a long history, breeders take the history of the parents seriously (especially the members of the different Corgi organizations). You will want to go over the complete history for both parents to get an idea of what you can expect from the puppies. From their personalities to their tendencies, you will be able to get a good idea of what you should expect from your newest family member.

You should spend a good bit of time learning about the parents from the breeder as well. The things that you want to know are probably found in stories about the parents more than from a website that details their lineage and history.

Selecting Your Puppy

Selecting a Corgi puppy is pretty much the same as picking any kind of puppy. A lot of it is entirely up to you and what you want in a dog. The

Photo Courtesy of
Caitlin Cassity

experience can be highly entertaining and enjoyable – and ultimately very difficult. As much fun as it is, you do need to be careful and serious so that you are not swayed by things that you may find bothersome later.

As you look over the puppies, notice how well each puppy plays with the others. This is a great indicator of just how well your puppy will react to any pets you already have at home.

You also need to look at the puppies as a group. If you notice that a majority of the puppies exhibit aggressive behavior or seem to tend toward being mistrustful, you may not want to select a puppy from that litter. Similarly, if the puppies appear to be terrified of you, such as keeping their tails tucked or shrinking away (since you cannot tell with the Pembroke's stubby tail if the puppy is trying to tuck it), that is an indication of the kinds of issues you may encounter with your puppy and its training. What you want is a litter that is full of friendly puppies, even if they do not start to greet you immediately. Sometimes they just want to play with their siblings or figure out what is happening first.

Next, notice that there is often at least one who is very eager to meet you. Many people take that as a sign that that puppy is the right one for their family. However, that is not always the case. Keep in mind that the puppy or puppies that greet you are more forward and demanding than the ones who sit back and analyze the situation first.

The puppies who hang back may be afraid, or, more likely, they just want to understand the situation before they get involved. They are not the alpha types that their eager siblings are. These are your more patient and tame puppies, ones who may be easier to train.

Pick the puppy that exhibits the personality traits that you want in your dog. If you want a forward, friendly, excitable dog, the first one to greet you may be the one you seek. If you want a dog that will think things through and let others get more attention, the mellower dog may be better for your home.

Adopting an Older Dog

The one thing that is universal about puppies is that they are a lot of work. If you miss a day or two of training it may feel like you are back to square one. Older Corgis can offer you a way to get your Corgi without having to dedicate several years to training. You can find older Corgis in shelters, rescues, and even from breeders. Breeders will take back puppies if a person does not treat the dog right or if a person can no longer take care of the Corgi for some reason.

Benefits

Older dogs give you more immediate gratification. You don't have to go through those sleepless nights with the new puppy or the endless frustration that comes with early types of training. Older Corgis let you get right into enjoying your dog as you go out on adventures. All intelligent, high energy dogs require a lot of time and attention as puppies. Bypassing that is a major part of the appeal of older dogs.

Older Corgis not only have the basic training already done, many of them already know some tricks, so you can start exploring the world of what they know and what they still have to learn. This is an incredibly fun, funny, and enjoyable experience, just like getting to know a new friend. You can also start your own training. This part is nearly as much fun because older Corgis have the attention span and ability to learn incredibly fast (if they are in the mood), and you will be able to recognize when they are learning and when they are uninterested in the activity.

Better still, they can help you start improving yourself. If you want to get more exercise, an older Corgi will help you get started immediately (instead of trapping you at home trying to teach it the basics). You also have a wide range of possible activities, and your Corgi will be more than happy to join you as you explore new places or get a new look at old ones.

Adult Corgis are ideal for individuals and families who do not have the time or patience to work with a puppy.

Photo Courtesy of
Kandace Wilkens

Rescues

The Corgi clubs have their own rescues, in addition to their own breeders. You are not as likely to find this breed outside of the small clique because Corgi people are very adamant about how the dogs should be taken care of – and they take care of their own. Corgis that you get through the organizations and breeders have most of the necessary information that is required to sell puppies, meaning you will have the medical history and vaccination information on the dog (although if the human parent was negligent or abusive, the medical history and information may not have been tracked while the dog was with them).

It is very easy to contact the organization to see about adopting an adult Corgi. They will require you to apply for the adoption simply because they want to ensure that the dog gets a great home – a place where the dog will be able to happily live out the rest of its days. They will also try to match you up with an adult dog who is ideal for the environment you offer and the lifestyle you live.

If you are interested in an adult Pembroke Welsh Corgi, you can visit the Pembroke Welsh Corgi Club site for details.

If you prefer a Cardigan Welsh Corgi, check out the Cardigan Welsh Corgi National Rescue Trust for more information.

Photo Courtesy of Janet Maddox

Warning about Small Children and Other Pets

Adult Corgis already have an established personality, and that personality may not go well with young children and other pets. While they do not tend to be aggressive dogs, some Corgis can be territorial. They are not inclined to backing down, either (they couldn't when facing off against cattle), and this may not go well if you already have a territorial dog at home, or a dog with an alpha personality.

Young kids are a different problem because adult Corgis may not have been raised around kids. This could lead to them being less patient with the squeals and rough play of younger kids. They may also be inclined to nipping at the heels of children if that characteristic was not trained out of them at an early age. It isn't that they want to hurt the kids, they just want to herd and corral the kids, a behavior that can scare children.

Choosing Between the Pembroke and the Cardigan

One of the best things about adopting an adult Corgi is that its personality is already established. That means you will be able to find out if the older dog lives up to the common personalities of the two types.

- The Pembroke tends to be friendlier and happier, making it easy to involve them in the things that you do, no matter where you are. You can ask the rescuers if the adult is more like a typical Pembroke to find out which of the adult dogs most closely exhibits the kind of personality you want.

- Cardigans are more intelligent, deliberate, and protective. That means you can ask if the rescued dog has the characteristics that are required for a more sedentary lifestyle (although it should not be too sedentary – it just saves you from having to keep the dog entertained at all times).

It will be considerably easier to find the dog that matches the personality you want since the dog's personality is already established. You can also ask if the problems common to the two types will be an issue so you know if you should plan to start training or if you should keep looking for a different adult Corgi.

CHAPTER 5

Preparing for Your Puppy

There is a lot of excitement that builds up when waiting for your Corgi puppy to come home. There is also a lot of work that you need to do to ensure that you are ready to take on the responsibilities of being a puppy parent. With a small, smart, high-energy puppy, you are going to have your hands full keeping your puppy out of trouble. The best way to do that is to puppy-proof your home starting a month or more before the puppy arrives.

Preparing Your Kids

Photo Courtesy of Gayla Miller

The initial preparation starts as soon as you decide to get a Corgi puppy. Your kids will probably be the ones spending the most time with the puppy, and that means you need to make sure they know how to behave around the puppy and handle it properly. Once the puppy arrives, it will be too late to try to introduce proper behavior.

The best thing to do is to have the rules and responsibilities assigned before the puppy is even old enough to arrive. You will need to refresh these points several times, including the day when the puppy arrives.

As the kids start to play with the puppy, you will be able to firmly remind your children how to behave if they start to get too rough or excited with the puppy.

Here are the five golden rules your kids should understand before the puppy comes home:

1. You must play gently. Their fluff ball appearance is deceptive in that it hides how fragile and small Corgi puppies actually are. There is not time when playing roughly with a young puppy is okay.

2. You must have firm rules about what will happen if your children begin to be too rough. A puppy who nips and bites when a child plays rough is not the party at fault – it is the child's fault. Make sure your child understands this for safe and peaceful play time.

3. Chase is an outside game. When the children go outside with the puppy and an adult, chase may be fine (if the puppy is up for it). It is never acceptable inside the home. Running inside the home creates one of two dangerous impressions on a puppy – either it learns that they are not safe even inside, or it learns that running in the home is fine. You do not want your adult Corgi barreling through the home knocking people over because this was considered acceptable when the Corgi was little.

4. Leave the puppy alone at meal time. This is meant to address when the puppy is eating (although you can apply it to when your children are eating too since you don't want your Corgi thinking that your food is fair game). You do not want the puppy to feel insecure about eating. Corgi puppies are not likely to create too much trouble if children disturb them, but you really don't want your dog feeling like its food needs to be defended too. That is unfair to the dog. And old Corgis are protective, resulting in biting if the Corgi learned to fend for its food at an early age.

5. Leave the puppy on the ground. Make sure to explain this to younger children especially. People want to pick up and play with puppies, but it is incredibly uncomfortable for the puppy. Kids will want to treat the puppy like a baby, and this can make the puppy both uncomfortable and fearful. The younger the child, the harder it will be for them to handle a squirming puppy. When the kids find out that the puppy has a very hard nip or bite, it is not the puppy's fault – kids should not be picking up the puppy in the first place. There are plenty of fun activities that can be enjoyed on the ground, so kids should leave the puppy there to play. Remember to apply this rule to yourself as well so that you are setting a good example.

6. Keep anything you value out of your children's reach. There is really no age where your valuables are safe when it comes to kids and puppies. Even teenagers are likely to grab things that they should know better than to use to play with a puppy. Curiosity leads to kids not

thinking about whether or not they should present something to the puppy. If you don't want your children and puppy to destroy something, make sure it is never on hand to destroy.

Preparing Your Current Dogs

Once your kids understand the rules, you have to start preparing your current dogs for the soon-to-arrive puppy. Of course, you will need a completely different approach as your dog or dogs are not going to understand you sitting down and trying to lay out the rules for them.

Here is how you can start to prepare your other dogs for the new arrival:

- Assess your dog's personality. If your dog has never had trouble with other dogs, you are probably fine. If your dog has ever shown territorial tendencies, you will need to be very careful. If your dog is excitable, you will need to think of ways to help calm your dog so that it does not get too rough with the puppy.

- Think of times when you have had other dogs over to your home. If your dog was territorial, this could be a sign that you will need to be extra careful when introducing the new puppy into your home.

Photo Courtesy of
Kandace Wilkens

If you have never had another dog over, you might consider inviting a friend with a dog or two over to gauge your dog's reaction. A dog's personality can be significantly different when out walking compared to being at home.

- Consider if you have seen your dog exhibit protective or possessive behavior. Food is the most common cause of possessive behavior, but dogs can also be possessive or protective about toys and people.

Make sure the space for the puppy is an area where your dog cannot go. Your new Corgi should not be interacting with other dogs without supervision. You will also need to ensure that none of your dog's stuff (including favorite chair or other furniture) is within the puppy's space.

Plan to have your dog meet the puppy for the first time outside of the home. Designate a spot that is neutral ground for the first meeting. This will ensure that your dog does not feel territorial upon meeting the puppy, giving them a chance to get to know each other a little.

Make sure that you have at least one other adult present for the initial meeting. This will ensure that you do not have to manage an excited dog and an energetic puppy by yourself. The alpha of the home or the two people who will be in charge of the dog and puppy should be present for this first encounter so that both your new puppy and your dog see the pack hierarchy of your home.

You may need to take the introductory period very slowly, depending on your dog's personality. It may take you a week to get the dog and puppy acclimated to each other. Remember that you are completely changing the dynamic of the home, and your dog may not be too pleased with this. If your dog is older, this could be incredibly difficult, and there are good odds that the dog will take that frustration out on the puppy. Make sure they are both safe and happy before leaving them to regularly interact.

If you have multiple dogs, all of these rules still apply. You will need to consider the personality of each dog and carefully monitor its behavior with the puppy. The introduction may need to be done with one dog at a time so that you do not overwhelm the puppy. Introducing each dog one at a time will help them calm down a bit before bringing all of the dogs together at one time.

Dangerous Foods

There are a lot of foods that people eat that are dangerous or deadly to dogs. Some of these foods are well-known (even to those who never had a dog), while others come as a surprise.

You really have your work cut out for you with Corgis, though, because they love to eat. The following is a list of foods that you need to make sure your Corgi can never get to as they are potentially fatal if consumed by a dog.

- Apple seeds
- Chocolate
- Coffee
- Cooked bones (they can kill when they splinter in the dog's mouth or stomach)
- Corn on the cob (it is the cob that is deadly to dogs, corn off the cob is fine, but you need to make sure that your Corgi cannot reach any corn that is still on the cob)
- Grapes/raisins
- Macadamia nuts
- Onions and chives
- Peaches, persimmons, and plums
- Tobacco (your Corgi will not know that it is not a food and may eat it if it is left out)
- Xylitol (a sugar substitute in candies and baked goods)
- Yeast

In addition to these potentially deadly foods, there is a long list of things that your dog shouldn't eat for health reasons. The Canine Journal has a lengthy list of foods that should be avoided. It includes things like alcohol and other things that people give dogs thinking it is funny. Remember that dogs have a very different metabolism and the effect that these foods have on them is much stronger than the effect on people.

For the sake of your Corgi's health, it is best just to keep all of these foods out of reach, even if they are non-lethal.

Hazards to Fix

Your home is full of things that are potentially dangerous to your Corgi. Preparing your home is going to be a relatively time-consuming endeavor, but ultimately a worthwhile one as it will help you keep your puppy safe.

You should start puppy-proofing your home at least a month before you bring your new Corgi home. The following will help you get an idea of what you will need to do, although there may be more or less to do depending on your home.

Kitchen and Eating Areas

The kitchen has plenty of dangerous things in it besides food. Easily the most life-threatening things in the kitchen are the poisons and cleaning supplies. Just as you would secure them from a small child, you have to secure them from your Corgi puppy. Keep in mind they are exceptionally intelligent dogs, and at some point they will likely figure out how to get into your cabinets if you do not puppy-proof them.

You will also need to be vigilant in putting away the poisons. Leaving them up on countertops is not safe because no matter how small your Corgi seems, there is still potential for that little pup to get up on the counter tops through means you never considered. At no time should you leave poisons in an unsecured place in your kitchen.

The trashcan is also transformed from a trash receptacle into a potential danger. Anything you put in it can be dug out by a Corgi if you do not take necessary precautions. You can lock the trashcan up in a pantry or cabinet, or you can get a locking trashcan. Whatever you choose, make sure that the trashcan is always locked where your Corgi cannot explore it.

You will need to make sure there are no electrical cords around the kitchen that the Corgi can pull or trip on. You do not want to have your blender pulled off of the counter and smashed on the floor because the cord was dangling over the side of the counter. The same thing applies to the cords on blinds. Keep them well off of the ground and out of reach of your Corgi.

Bathroom and Laundry

You will need to do the same puppy-proofing in the bathroom as the kitchen. The poisons must always be stored where the puppy cannot reach them, and the trashcans locked so that they cannot be explored.

Keep the toilet closed too. Corgi puppies can do things you would not expect, so make sure they cannot get into the toilet. Never use automatic toilet cleaners. In the event that someone leaves the toilet lid up, your Corgi is going to try to drink from it. Make sure when that happens that your dog is not drinking poisons.

Your laundry area will need to be puppy-proofed as well, but usually it is considerably easier. For the most part, you need to make sure that there is no dirty laundry where your puppy or dog can reach it. It usually won't be dangerous, but you do not want your dog dragging dirty underclothing around the home. There will also be times when things will end up in the wash that have potentially poisonous substances on them (such as clothes that have bleach or oil). You need to get in the habit of keeping the dirty clothes out of your Corgi's reach. If you have a laundry room, the solution is to simply keep the door closed at all times. This will also keep you from the surprise emergency vet visit after your Corgi eats a sock or hose.

Other Rooms

Make sure that you keep cords out of reach, that there are no cleaning products around the home, and that any potentially dangerous objects are stored somewhere safe. If you have a fireplace, make sure all of the cleaning supplies and tools are somewhere that your Corgi cannot get to them to play. You also need to keep the place where the fire is closed off so that your Corgi cannot get into it.

For stairs, use a gate to keep your Corgi from falling down them. For tables, make sure you do not leave anything dangerous, such as scissors or sewing supplies, where your puppy can climb up to them. Pens, pencils, and other tools need to be kept out of reach, as well as valuables and anything you don't want your Corgi to chew.

For cat owners, the litter box needs to be stored somewhere that your cat can go but your Corgi cannot. This likely means teaching your cat to use the litter box in a new place, so make sure you move the box well ahead of the puppy's arrival. This will keep you from having a cat who has two reasons to be angry at you.

Garage

Garages are a place of excitement and danger for Corgis. With all of the chemicals and hazardous items, your Corgi should never be left alone in the garage. Of course, you probably cannot keep your Corgi from ever being in the garage either (at least when you take your puppy somewhere, it will pass through the garage). This means you will need to take the time to puppy-proof it as well.

Photo Courtesy of
Virginia Godwin

All tools, equipment, and items related to car maintenance (or any-thing with an engine or wheels) needs to be stored somewhere with a lock. This includes things like leaf blowers and bike tools. Your puppy is just as likely to try to chew on a bike tire as to lap up antifreeze or try to roll around in fertilizer. Keep all of these somewhere the puppy cannot go.

Fishing equipment also needs to be organized and stored in a place where your puppy cannot reach it. It can be in a closet or high on a shelf. If you store it up high, make sure there is no way to climb up to it. Do not leave any part of the equipment dangling over the side of the counter.

You should step back and examine your garage from the perspective of a toddler, then get down and look at it from a Corgi's angle. Anything that looks like it could attract attention and cause problems needs to be moved well out of reach.

Outdoors and Fencing

Never leave your Corgi puppy outside alone. Too many things can happen when your puppy is unsupervised. Even if you have a fence, you cannot leave the little pup outside without someone watching at all times.

It won't take you as long to puppy-proof the outside as the inside, but you should still plan for it to take an hour or two as you are going to be looking at things in a whole new way.

Inspect the fence to make sure there are no breaks, holes, or potential problems. Make sure there are no gaps under the bottom for your Corgi to tunnel under. If you see any gaps, holes, or broken areas, get them fixed before the puppy arrives. Your Corgi will try to get through these as soon as it notices them, and that is dangerous in the event that your Corgi either escapes or gets stuck.

Select an area you want your Corgi to use as a bathroom. Once you know where you want your puppy to go, make sure there is nothing poisonous or dangerous in the area. Even a birdbath is a potential danger, so select the area well.

Select a different area for playing to help your Corgi know when you expect business to get done and when it is time to play. Your Corgi will learn fast. Give the play area the same inspection that you gave the area to be used for the bathroom.

Walk around your yard and make sure all chemicals and potentially dangerous tools are moved out of reach. If you have a shed, lock it up, and make sure the Corgi cannot enter.

Make sure none of the plants in your yard are a danger to your dog. There are good odds that your puppy is going to chew on them, so make sure there is no potential for danger when it happens.

Make sure all water areas, such as pools and small ponds, are secured. Your fire ring or pit and grill need to be secure so that your puppy cannot play in them.

Photo Courtesy of
Michele Eathorne

Walk around your yard and think of it from the perspective of a small child. This will help you identify other potential dangers that need to be addressed before the puppy arrives.

Supplies and Tools to Purchase and Prepare

You need to have everything purchased and ready before your puppy arrives. Even the most basic list is quite extensive, so start shopping a month or two in advance. The following lists the basics:

- Crate
- Bed
- Leash
- Doggie waste bags for walks
- Collar
- Tags
- Puppy food
- Water and food bowls (sharing a water bowl is usually okay, but your puppy needs its own food dish if you have multiple dogs)
- Toothbrush
- Brush
- Toys

If you think of anything that you would like to get, add it to the list. This could include things like flea treatments for when your puppy reaches the age that you need to start treatments.

Training tools and treats need to be on your list, so know how you plan to train your dog, including housetraining. If you plan to start training indoors, you will need the right equipment. Training (both house and behavior) will begin that first week when your puppy arrives, so you need to have everything ready beforehand.

Also, if you plan to train your Corgi puppy to do agility courses, then you may want to pick up a few of the basics. It will be a little early the first couple of months to start training, but before you know it, your Corgi is going to be ready for something new and exciting, and agility courses can give your puppy the excitement and exercise that will keep it too tired to misbehave.

Planning the First Year's Budget

Puppies may not be as expensive as children, but they can still cost a considerable amount of money. This means you need to create a budget so that you have adequate funds available for all of the essentials, such as regular vet visits and shots, food, and supplies.

It is a given that you are going to end up spending more than you plan on, so try to build a cushion into your Corgi supply budget.

The best time to start your puppy budget is the day you decide to get a puppy. In all likelihood, you are going to need to spend a good bit of time researching the things you will need to do over that first year. Vets have different prices between cities and states, so you will need to find out which one has a great reputation and how much it will cost for each visit that first year. There are a lot of things that Corgis can do, so if you want to get involved in an organization, or even just basic dog training, you will need to conduct research.

Puppies can be a lot more expensive than most people realize. That is why you need to start budgeting immediately and make sure you have done your homework well ahead of your Corgi's arrival.

Keep Things out of Reach

This is incredibly important to understand when you bring a Corgi into your home. They are not only smart, they are far more agile than you would expect with that stout little body. This is a breed that can win agility contests, and it clearly isn't because of its sleek athletic build. This breed is smart and knows how to use its stout figure to do stuff you would not expect.

A Short Story on Their Intelligence and Problem Solving

There was a family who had a Corgi and noticed that food had been disappearing from the table. They had no idea how this was happening, so they filmed the kitchen to see what was going on.

Enter their Corgi.

The dog moved the kitchen chair out from under the table, hopped up on the chair, and easily reached the food. Once the dog was done eating, it was time to hide the evidence. Once on the ground, the Corgi pushed the chair back under the table.

Corgis know what they want, and they are always looking for ways to get it. If you don't want your Corgi snacking on your food or getting into dangerous stuff, the only way to really secure your stuff is to keep it in a place where the Corgi cannot reach--or get to by moving something. Usually locks are the easiest way to go.

Clearly, out of reach for a Corgi is entirely different than it is with nearly any other breed. Not all Corgis are so focused and determined, but it is better to err on the side of caution and make sure you don't inadvertently leave a puzzle for your Corgi to solve. Your Corgi is not being a bad dog – it is being the incredibly clever creature that it has been bred to be. Also, your Corgi does not like being alone and does not like to be bored. Making sure that these two things don't happen often (and certainly don't happen at the same time) will do a lot to help. However, the best solution is to always keep things somewhere safe if you don't want your Corgi to get them.

Photo Courtesy of Cassie Thwaites

Summary

With a Corgi, it is a constant game of out-thinking your dog. Your puppy will be incredibly fun, but there will be a whole lot of learning in those first few months. To make sure you aren't distracted, have everything set up well ahead of your puppy's arrival.

Don't forget to prepare your other pets too. It is going to be a very stressful time for them, and you want to let them know that you still care about them; you are just adding to the family. You will need to plan to spend alone time with your current pets after the puppy gets home too. If you build that into the schedule now, your pets will be less anxious later when it is obvious that the schedule is not entirely different.

Photo Courtesy of
Sunny Hanford

CHAPTER 6

The First Week

Photo Courtesy of
Cindy Duwe

Once you get your Corgi puppy home, pretty much everything changes. It is an experience that you will never forget. Starting with a puppy means starting with all of the potential that your puppy has – it is a commitment to making sure your Corgi is raised and trained in a way that will make your dog happy and healthy.

Those first seven days establish a lot about the kind of environment the puppy will be living in, the first steps of turning that potential into your perfect dog. Now that you have completed all of the puppy-proofing, you get to start on the fun stuff – the care, training, and fun of owning a Corgi.

Preparation and Planning

The time to start is actually before your puppy arrives – the planning and preparation. You need to make sure you have everything set up for your Corgi so that you are not trying to figure everything out as you go (you will be doing enough of that as it is).

Start with one final check to ensure that you have adequately puppy-proofed your home. Corgi puppies are small, so you may need to get down on the floor to see your home from their angle. This should be done over the course of the week before your puppy comes home.

Have a list of everything your puppy will need right from the start. That list should include (but won't be limited to) the following:

55

- Food
- Bed
- Crate
- Toys
- Water and food dishes
- Leash
- Collar
- Treats

Photo Courtesy of
Caitlin Cassity

If you plan to fence your puppy into a particular area of your abode, you will also need gates and items to make sure your Corgi cannot get out of the designated puppy space. You should have everything on this list before the puppy gets to your home because you are not going to have time to go purchase them later (especially not on the first day you have your puppy).

Sit down with your family and make sure everyone understands the rules, especially children. They need to be trained in proper puppy handling, and you will need to be as strict with your kids as you are with your puppy when it comes to taking care of the newest family member. Make sure you know who is in charge of the basic puppy care (feeding and walking). Training should be everyone's job, but there will likely be a primary trainer as well. You can establish paired responsibility if your child or children want to help – one child and one adult who make sure the puppy gets the food and water required every day, for example.

Finally, plan on having a routine for your Corgi puppy. It is nearly certain that the plan will change, but you need to have somewhere to begin so that you are working the training and regular care into the day, every day. You can tweak the schedule as needed, but have a schedule you can work with before the puppy arrives. Once in your home, the puppy is going to be more than enough to occupy your time so that you will not have time to think about much else.

That last week before your puppy comes home, make sure you have everything planned and ready. It will never be quite enough, but it is much better than trying to wing it with an intelligent puppy that may be able to use your lack of planning to its own canine advantage.

The Ride Home

Training begins from the moment the Corgi puppy gets into your car. Everything that puppy needs to know happens during that first trip.

Yes, you will be tempted to cuddle and play and make exceptions to the rules, but that is exactly the kind of behavior that is going to undermine your training. Your puppy is learning about you from that first impression, and you want that impression to be that you are the one in charge. That adorable little face is backed by a lot of brains, and it is going to use what it learns during the first car ride to understand the nature of your relationship.

All intelligent working dogs require a firm, consistent hand from the very beginning – Corgis are no exception. The first ride helps the puppy to understand the structure and organization of the pack.

If possible, you should have two adults on the trip. Find out if the puppy has ever been in a vehicle before, and if not, make sure you have someone else present for that first ride. One person will drive, and the other will comfort the puppy. Even though Corgis are not prone to being afraid, cars are not a natural phenomenon and that first trip may be scary. Start teaching your puppy how enjoyable car rides can be.

If you plan on using a crate for the trip home, ensure that the puppy will be secure. You do not want the crate to shift and move with the Corgi inside of it. Being jostled and feeling powerless about it is not a great first impression of car trips.

First Night Frights

The first few nights away from Mommy can be intimidating, if not downright frightening. However, there is only so much you should do to help reassure your puppy because at some point the puppy learns that certain negative behaviors get results. It is a balancing act that will be difficult to get right, but will ultimately be worth it. Your job is to teach your puppy that nighttime is not so scary and that your home is safe.

If you want to keep your Corgi off of the beds, you have to start now. That means you cannot bring the puppy onto the bed at night. Once you allow your Corgi on the bed, there is no convincing that canine that you actually mean "no dogs on the bed".

There will be unfamiliar noises and sounds, and your Corgi puppy will hear each and every one of them. In return, your puppy will probably make a lot of noises too. These noises let you know the puppy is uncomfortable, afraid, or simply lonely. This is to be expected, considering the constant companionship that the puppy had at its previous home with Mommy and the siblings.

You cannot think of these noises as being bothersome to you, even though they will be (especially as you try to sleep). Do not move the puppy further away from you so that you can sleep better or be less annoyed. That will only frighten your puppy more, causing anxiety and reinforcing the fear of being in your home. No matter how much you are bothered by the noises, you must keep the puppy in the room with you during those first few terrifying nights. Over time, the puppy will be reassured and calmed simply by having you in the room.

Are you likely to get good sleep? Absolutely not. It's a lot like bringing home a human infant; this infant is just furrier and smaller. It's part of the deal when you decide on a Corgi puppy instead of an adult dog.

You should already have a designated sleeping area for your Corgi, whether a crate, pen, or bed. The area should definitely be set off from the rest of the room with boundaries that the puppy cannot escape (not for a little while, anyway). When your Corgi starts to make noise, you have to learn to ignore the noises. This will be extremely difficult, and extremely necessary. If you give in to the whimpering, whining, and crying now, the dog will expect that to work in the future (and will get louder with each time you try to ignore it later).

Finally, you need a plan for bathroom breaks. This may be a small area within the puppy's space, or it could be a trip outside every few hours (depending on how you want to house train your Corgi). Whatever your chosen housetraining path, you will need to get up to help your puppy several times during the night.

Photo Courtesy of
Liza Gagne

First Vet Visit

You should take your new puppy to the vet within a day or two of its arrival at your home. This will help you ensure that your puppy is healthy and will create a rapport between your Corgi and the vet. That initial assessment of your Corgi will help you learn more about your pet and will give you a chance to ask the vet for advice on anything that you are unsure of. This trip is the baseline by which your vet will gauge your puppy's growth and development.

The trip will certainly elicit emotions from your Corgi, whether excitement or anxiety. Odds are good that your Corgi will want to explore everything in the office, especially the other animals. After all, this is probably your Corgi's first chance at socialization with other animals outside of your home. Make sure to ask before your puppy approaches any of the other animals at the vet's office – you do not want the first encounter with another dog or cat to be horrifying. You want the other animal to be mellow or interested (though not too excited) about meeting the puppy. The owner will be able to tell you if it is alright, or warn you that it is not a good idea. Remember, the older animals may be sick and not feeling well. Introducing them to a puppy could be a risky idea.

Also, make sure to give your puppy positive feedback for good behavior at the office. Being comforting and affectionate will teach your puppy that the vet's office is not a bad place (something that they will probably learn after repeat visits of "torture"). Creating a positive environment will help your puppy learn to be at ease even when visiting the vet.

*Photo Courtesy of
Sunny Hanford*

The Start of Training

Training begins the moment the puppy gets into your car, and it will continue over the course of that first week. You will build on this training over the coming weeks and months.

This is the time to start minimizing the behaviors you do not want.

Nipping

Corgis are notorious nippers. As small dogs, they relied on their bite to get the point across with cattle that ignored their bark. There is a good chance that your puppy will start nipping during that first week. Be prepared to start correcting your puppy the first time it happens.

Barking

If you want your pet to be uncharacteristically quiet (for a Corgi), you must start during that first week when your puppy barks. It will probably mean a few extra treats, but that is how you will teach your Corgi what quiet is. Your puppy will also be noisy when trying to get your attention, so you will be training yourself to react in a certain way to the noise as well. Doing that now will be much easier than re-training yourself later.

Photo Courtesy of
Cassie Thwaites

The Leash

Leash training will probably be pretty easy since your Corgi will be excited about going outside. This training is actually just as much for you as for the puppy. You do not want to get used to dragging the puppy away from things that it is sniffing. You will need to start finding ways to keep your puppy walking without being too forceful.

Teaching Respect

With any smart dog, respect is essential to the training. You want to teach your puppy to respect you without fearing you. Consistency is the best way to do that. Do not make exceptions during the first week because you will be fighting to correct that lesson for the rest of your Corgi's life.

Acclimation to a Wide Range of Sounds

Your Corgi's exceptional hearing is going to be obvious right from the start. Watch those ears perk up and that face start to look for the source of the sound. You want to be with your puppy as much as possible, exposing your dog to as many sounds as you can. This will help your dog know which sounds are safe, reducing the puppy's anxiety while helping the puppy learn when it is okay to bark.

Grooming (They Shed; Get Used to Constant Grooming)

That beautiful dirt-resistant coat comes at a very high price – the shedding never stops.

You should get in the habit of brushing your puppy. Often. At least weekly, but even more if you want to fight the shedding that is about to go on in your home. This will help cut down on the amount of fur that will make its way all around your home, as well as teaching your puppy how to behave during grooming. You can rotate the responsibility between different people, making sure children are supervised when brushing the puppy. It should be an enjoyable and quick task that takes just a couple of minutes (as long as you groom often).

It isn't compulsory, though. If you are okay with having little balls of Corgi fur traveling around your home like tumbleweeds, all you have to do is stick to grooming your Corgi once a month or once a quarter – just be prepared for a whole lot more housework.

CHAPTER 7

The First Month

By the end of the first week, you are probably tired but already getting an idea what your puppy's personality is like. With an idea of what works (and what probably doesn't), you can spend the next month really working on training. Despite being an adorable little bundle of fun, your Corgi will let you know that you have your work cut out for you (as you saw during that first week).

As with most challenging tasks, when you successfully train a Corgi puppy, it is highly rewarding. The daily practice and training will start to yield results relatively quickly, helping to keep you motivated. The eager look on your puppy's face can be an even better motivator. And remember, when your Corgi is tired, there is no energy left to misbehave.

Keep this in mind over that first month.

Not up to Full Strength

Photo Courtesy of Jessica Burleski

Once your Corgi is an adult, you will be able to take your dog nearly anywhere to play, hike, and explore. Right now though, you are largely homebound. Of course, you will be able to go out to teach your puppy how to walk on a leash, but the excursions will generally be close to home for that first month. You will also need to break up the walks and exercise so that they are spread out over the course of the day (you can't take your puppy on two long walks – the little guy simply does not have the energy for that).

On the positive side, there will a lot of naps mixed into the day. That means after you head out for a walk, you can plan on getting some work done as your puppy crashes. However, you still need to keep your canine restricted to the puppy area. If you have bedding in the room where you will be working, that could be alright, as long as you plan to drop what you are doing as soon as the puppy wakes.

By the end of the month, you will probably notice that your Corgi is able to go a good bit further than it was able to in the beginning. You will need to adjust your routine to meet the needs of your Corgi. It could mean fewer walks that last nearly twice as long.

Setting the Rules and Sticking to Them

Photo Courtesy of Caitlin Cassity

Corgis like to have things their way, and given their incredibly cute demeanor and physique, they are quite accustomed to getting it. It is incredibly easy to feel that your new puppy isn't ready for the firm hand you know you will need later.

It's not true –they need it more now than they will later.

If you neglect to keep your puppy under control, you will find it next to impossible to gain control later. After all, you have already taught your puppy that you are not the one in control, and once that idea is in your Corgi's head, there's really nothing you can do to change the dog's mind.

You will be tempted to let it go.

Your puppy is going to try to convince you that it needs more attention, fewer rules, and more food, but you have to let your Corgi know that your way is the way of the house.

If you can get through that first month without giving into that feeling that just once won't hurt, you will have a much easier time with your Corgi. Your young, impressionable Corgi will learn to respect you from the very first month, and that makes all the difference in the world. You can start making exceptions much, much, much later (when your dog is around five or six years old). There is no point while your Corgi is a puppy that you should be making exceptions in training and rules.

Early Socialization

Corgis are very individualistic, and if they are not socialized, they can be little terrors. Early socialization is critical to ensuring that your Corgi is well behaved around other dogs and people. Socialization should be an activity that you focus on during the first month after your Corgi arrives.

If you have family and friends with dogs that are well socialized, make play dates with them. You can either have the dog over to your home, or you can take the puppy to the dog's home (unless the dog is territorial, then it is best to meet at your home or on neutral ground). Socialization could even be built into your walks if you know people nearby who are willing to walk their dogs with you and the puppy.

You also need to socialize your Corgi with people. This will proba-bly be easier since you just need people nearby who want to play with a puppy (yeah, pretty easy to find that). This can include small children, but you will need to be very careful. Because of a Corgi's sensitive hearing,

Photo Courtesy of
Tricia Pablo

65

Photo Courtesy of Jae Ojala

you want the children to be calm enough not to shout and make loud noises around the puppy. They also need to be old enough to understand to be gentle with the puppy. If a child is rough with a Corgi puppy, the Corgi is much more likely to nip and bite.

Strive to make socialization an activity that you do several times a week, or if you can manage it, make it a daily activity. The more you socialize your Corgi, the more activities you will be able to enjoy out and around the town, state, or country. Since they are travel-sized, you want to have a Corgi who will be happy to see people and other dogs, not one who is wary and snappy.

You should avoid dog parks at this stage. During that first month, there is a lot for your puppy to learn, and going to a dog park will expose your Corgi to a lot of things over which you have no control. At this point, you want the puppy's meetings and socializing to be in a controlled environment.

Do be kind to your older pets at this stage as well. They are going to need a break from the high-energy fur ball that does not understand limits and boundaries. Make sure your older pet has plenty of time away from the puppy over the course of the day. If your older pet is particularly irritable, it may be best to try to keep the two apart most (if not all) of the time.

Treats and Rewards vs. Punishments

When people think about dog training, treats are one of the first things to come to mind, followed quickly by punishments for puppies in the early stages. There are problems with both of these courses of action, and you cannot rely on just one way to train your puppy. It is a balancing act to make sure your puppy learns when something is a good behavior, and when it is unacceptable behavior.

When it comes to Corgis, though, positive reinforcement is far better – especially positive reinforcement that comes in the shape of more attention, activity, and toys.

All you have to do is look at a Corgi to see how dangerous it is for the pup to gain weight. You do not want to rely on treats to train your new family member (just as you don't teach children with a constant stream of candy and sweets). Treats should be given sparingly, and other forms

Photo Courtesy of Cindy Duwe

67

of positive reinforcement given freely and often. After all, you don't want your Corgi to learn to listen to you only when there is food involved.

Teaching your puppy that you are the alpha and that you should be respected is the best way of making other positive reinforcements more effective. Corgis want the alpha to be happy with them. If they respect you, most training will be unbelievably easy.

Occasional punishments may be necessary, especially for nipping. Keep in mind that the crate should never be used as a way of punishing your dog. It is meant to be a safe space that is your dog's refuge, not a prison. Instead, place the puppy in a time out where it can see you, but cannot interact with you. Then you need to ignore the puppy no matter how much barking, whining, or whimpering it does to get your attention. If you are seen as the top of the pack, this will be more painful than any other form of punishment. It is nearly impossible to overstate just how much Corgis want to be with their people. Denying them access while still being able to see you is a stark reminder of just why they need to behave in a certain way.

Exercise – Encouraging Staying Active

Your puppy may not be up for those long walks quite yet, but that does not mean that your puppy wants to sit around the house. This is the perfect opportunity for you to start being more aware of how sedentary you are.

Don't worry, you will want to exercise your puppy, if for no other reason than that you can have a few minutes of peace after the exercise is done. Make the time to play with your puppy, whether inside or outside, so that you can be sure that when your puppy is an adult it will be accustomed to moving and exercising. This is absolutely critical for Corgis since they can start to gain weight later in life if they do not get enough exercise.

Be creative in the kinds of activities you do (keeping in mind that your puppy is still a puppy). There will be things that your new family member won't understand, like fetch. You can still start to train, just don't be too pushy. That puppy is smart, and when it is ready, it will learn to bring the toy back to you instead of running away with it.

Other people and dogs can be great helpers when it comes to puppy training – especially adult dogs. Things are much easier for the puppy to understand when an adult dog does it first.

Make sure that the leash is a good fit. Your Corgi probably isn't going to be able to break it (unless it is an old, frayed leash), but they can be incredibly fast when it comes to working their way out of collars and leashes and taking off. You can bring this up with the vet to make sure the collar is adequately tight without choking your Corgi.

Activities Based on Breed

Keeping your Corgi active is relatively easy, but the two types tend to do better with activities that are more to their respective liking. Keeping in mind that every Corgi is different, the following can help you figure out what kinds of activities your Corgi is likely to enjoy during the first month. That way you can plan for it and get the right equipment to start training.

Keep in mind the fact that this is not true for all of them – there are Pembrokes that prefer to stay home and Cardigans that want nothing more than to be out doing things. Ultimately, you need to tailor the activates to your Corgi's interests and abilities. During the first month, you can help shape that personality, but you will be working with the foundation that is already there.

Photo Courtesy of
Michele Eathorne

Pembroke

Pembrokes love to have a purpose, even when they are young. You can start training them to participate in performance events, even during the first month. Remember that they are still puppies, so you shouldn't set your expectations too high –this is about having fun and tiring your puppy out. The Pembroke Corgi is incredibly agile, and you can start getting a good look at what it can do during that first month living with you.

This also serves the purpose of giving you an idea of just how much you have to pay attention to your dog over the coming months and years. Once you get an idea of how high it can jump and other surprising feats, you will start looking at your home in an entirely new light. This is good because you will probably need to start making adjustments to keep the growing dog from getting into things that it shouldn't get into.

Pembrokes are also great therapy dogs. While a puppy isn't going to be able to do much, you can start taking the puppy places to socialize where it will also be of some assistance. Make sure you are not over-straining your Corgi, though, as too much attention and stimulation can be overwhelming.

Photo Courtesy of
Jessi Hall

Cardigan

Cardigans tend to be more content at home. Focusing on training and fun activities that help you bond can be all your Cardigan Corgi needs. Hide and Seek is a fantastic game you can play with your puppy either in the house or in the yard. Being with you and getting your attention probably makes your Cardigan happier than being out and meeting new people.

Fetch may also be a rewarding activity for Cardigans as they get your full attention and get to make you happy.

CHAPTER 8

Housetraining

Easily one of the most tedious and painful lessons you will have to teach your puppy, housetraining is nonetheless one of the most important lessons your puppy will learn. With a Corgi, at least you know that it should be a relatively easy task since your dog is certainly intelligent enough to understand quickly.

To get started, you need to implement two rules.

1. The puppy is not to roam freely when no one is around to monitor it. Your Corgi is not going to want to be in a soiled crate, so there is very low risk of an accident when your puppy is crated or in a small enclosure once housetraining starts.

2. Your puppy should have constant, easy access to the location where you plan to do the training. Alternatively, you need to be prepared for frequent trips outside while your puppy is learning.

Once you understand and are ready to enforce these rules, you have a few decisions to make.

Photo Courtesy of Michele Eathorne

Understanding Your Dog

Photo Courtesy of Jennifer Durward

Corgis are incredibly individualistic, and that means you have to understand your puppy to properly train it. Just because a Corgi doesn't use the bathroom outside does not mean your dog does not understand – it probably means that your Corgi has found a more convenient alternative. If you are not consistent and firm, housetraining can be incredibly frustrating.

If your Corgi likes freedom, a doggie door is probably your best bet. If your Corgi prefers to go outside with you, outside training on the leash is probably the way to go. If you decide to train in the home with puppy pads, just be aware that you need to be prepared to move to outside training quickly. You do not want your dog thinking that it is an option to use the bathroom inside instead of going outside. Trying to correct that misunderstanding will be an ongoing headache.

Another cool thing about Corgis is that they like their space clean, so once they start understanding housetraining, they will let you know when they need to go outside. Your job is to learn the signs so that your Corgi can make it outside in time. This may conflict with the schedule you have chosen, but that is alright since the schedule is meant to help the Corgi understand where it is supposed to go to the bathroom. Once it is obvious that the Corgi understands the where, it can start letting you know when.

Inside or Outside

While you will want to move your Corgi to going to the bathroom outside as quickly as possible, it may be necessary to start with indoor training (for example, if your puppy comes home in the winter and it is too cold to go outside frequently). If you do begin inside, you have to make sure the puppy quickly learns that the only place where it is acceptable is in the space you designate.

If you start by training outdoors, be prepared to take your puppy out a lot, even at night during what would otherwise be regular sleeping hours. It will be time consuming, but fortunately this will only be for a short period of time as your Corgi will learn pretty quickly. If you have an area picked out where you want your Corgi to go, it will be easy to teach this at the beginning. Then you won't have to spend lots of time cleaning up your yard every week (at least not from your Corgi's waste). If you want to do this, you need to make sure to train it from the beginning, otherwise your Corgi is not likely to listen to you when you try to shrink the space it has for using the bathroom.

Using a leash can help you keep your puppy focused, as well as making it easy to show your dog where to go.

Establish Who Is Boss – Kind But Firm

You have to make sure to be firm and consistent when housetraining. There will be times where you will want to say "Good enough," but you can't. Once you do, your Corgi is going to apply that logic every time.

You have to let your Corgi know that you are the one making the rules. That means you have to enforce them at all times.

This is where regular bathroom breaks are necessary. When your puppy is able to anticipate the break, it will be easier for it to follow your rules.

Photo Courtesy of Tammie Songer

Positive Reinforcement – It's about Respect

You want your Corgi puppy to learn to respect you. Once your puppy learns you are the boss and respects your rules, positive reinforcement will be the best reward your Corgi could ask for, even better than treats (at least most of the time).

Your Corgi is going to want to do things the way it sees fit. If your puppy does not learn to respect you, then there is very little reason for it to take you seriously when you try to train it.

A positive relationship will build the trust and respect needed to prepare your Corgi for housetraining and beyond. Your Corgi just wants to have clear boundaries when it comes to knowing who runs the pack. Knowing that, the next important thing is knowing where he or she falls in the pack hierarchy, which includes other family members and pets. With you etablished as the alpha, your rules are what the Corgi will follow.

This makes it easy for you and other members of the family to train your puppy because it will learn to listen to you and others.

Punishing a Corgi for accidents is discouraged. It is unlikely that your Corgi will tie the accident to the punishment, so the lesson you are trying to teach is not going to be what your puppy takes away from the experience.

Corgis are people pleasers – they want to enjoy time with you. Positive reinforcement in the form of attention is easily one of the best motivators during housetraining.

Regular Schedule, Doggie Door, or Newspaper

The last question to ask yourself is how you plan to train your Corgi puppy. Much of the answer is going to depend on if you will start training inside or if you will do outside-only training.

Corgis tend to use the bathroom after a few specific events:

- After waking up (in the morning or after a nap)
- After being in a crate for a few hours
- When on the leash

Pay attention to when your Corgi is more likely to need to use the bathroom. This can help you quickly teach your puppy to use the outside.

Puppies do have smaller bladders and less control over them. If you need to start the training inside, make sure to get your puppy to the designated space as quickly as possible after the events that are likely to trigger a bathroom break. You will need to transition as quickly as possible.

You can also teach your puppy to use the bathroom when you are out walking. This could be done even in the backyard with leash training.

It's All on You – Corgis Like It Clean

Corgis are a clean breed and they do not like for their home to be soiled. Your job is to teach the Corgi that the entire inside is the home, and that the only acceptable place to use the bathroom is outside. If your

Photo Courtesy of Janet Maddox

Corgi does not get this, the vast majority of the time the trainer is at fault, not the Corgi. It is a sign that the trainer was not consistent, firm, or positive enough in the training approach. Corgis are stubborn, but they do understand when that stubbornness has no place in the home. If they feel comfortable being stubborn about using the bathroom inside, then you need to examine where you went wrong in the training. Then you will need to fix the problem to ensure your Corgi finally learns that only the outside is an acceptable place for bathroom breaks.

CHAPTER 9

Socialization and Experience

Intelligent working dogs need to be socialized early on because many of them tend to be territorial, and this includes Corgis. Your Corgi can be a lot of fun when it comes to playing, but if not properly socialized, the dog can either turn into a little terror or can be potentially terrorized by the most innocuous things.

You have to plan to socialize your Corgi starting from the day your puppy comes home. Without socialization, no amount of training is going to help your Corgi interact with other animals and humans. It is also important to remain firm even when you are socializing your Corgi because the rules still apply.

Photo Courtesy of
MaryAnn Carney

Benefits of Socialization

For Corgis, socialization is very important. They can be fantastic dogs, but they need a bit of guidance when it comes to dealing with other creatures (even humans). They can also get to be very skittish if they are left alone at home most of the time. Getting out and doing things helps them learn that the world is a safe place, so they do not need to be anxious.

Corgi Sensitivity

Corgis can hear things that most other animals cannot. This can make them prone to being anxious when they do not understand the source of a sound. For your puppy's sake, you should be getting it familiar with a lot of sounds to help it see what is creating the different noises it hears when it is inside.

It is also a lot of fun to watch Corgis interact with other dogs. When properly socialized, they can be the star of any dog park or gathering because they will show the same love and attention to everyone.

Problems Arising from Lack of Socialization

One of the primary potential problems with Corgis is that they have extraordinary hearing. Some Corgis will learn to be terrified of every little sound they hear because they have not been exposed to enough diversity to know otherwise. By going outside often and teaching it how to interact with the world, you are showing your Corgi that the world is a fun place, not a place to be feared. While it may not work to reduce the barking, it will certainly help to relieve some of the stress and anxiety when the noises it hears are familiar.

An anxious Corgi can be either very afraid or very aggressive, neither of which are healthy. It may also be more inclined to nip or bite.

Your Challenges with an Aggressive, Protective Dog

It is easy to think that a Corgi cannot do much harm because of its size, but that is not true, especially with children. If a Corgi is not socialized, that could make the dog far more aggressive, and that could create a very unhealthy relationship between your dog and the rest of the world. You do not want to have to keep your dog locked away because of aggressive behavior outside of the home.

Corgis want to protect you, which can be fine if you are at home and someone is breaking into the house. When you are out of the home, however, or having people over for company, this kind of behavior is completely unacceptable. Drawing the line between the two is much harder if you do not socialize your Corgi. Your canine should be able to enjoy the company of others instead of being locked up for fear of it biting or attacking visitors.

Why Genetics Matter

Genetics are significant because some Corgis are more inclined to aggressive or fearful behavior. Knowing the temperament of the parents will help you determine if a puppy is likely to have the right personality for your home. If the parents are skittish or standoffish, your puppy will be far more inclined to display the same personality traits.

A Strong Willed, But Loyal Dog

Corgis are undoubtedly a strong-willed dog, but they are also extremely loyal. They hate to be left alone without you for long periods of time and want to make sure that you are safe.

Corgis aren't known for being particularly aggressive, but there are some that can be. And most Corgis are prone to nipping, which you will need to train your dog out of as early as possible. All of this requires adequate time around other dogs and people.

*Photo Courtesy of
Dawn Blanchard*

The best way to use your dog's love, affection, and protection is to make sure your dog knows when aggressive or willful behavior is acceptable. By making a clear distinction, you can help your Corgi enjoy the world without being constantly wary of everything.

A large part of this is making sure your Corgi knows that you are the alpha of the home. A firm and consistent approach to training will go a long way, as will frequent socialization.

Common Problems

Barking is easily one of the most common problems people report about Corgis. It seems like they are constantly letting you know that there was a sound that you missed, which can be particularly challenging when you have guests over or when you are just out for a walk. Socialization can help reduce the amount of barking you endure by making your Corgi more aware of the sources of the sounds.

Nipping is also a commonly reported problem because it was what they did for centuries to get cattle where they needed to be.

Their destructive tendencies can quickly get old when you find that you cannot leave your Corgi home alone without losing something. Corgis hate to be alone, so it could be that they need a companion, in which case socialization is essential to ensure your pets do not fight in your home. Having another pet can help ease some of the boredom and restlessness.

Finally, Corgis have been called bossy. This does not mean that they try to dominate or be the alpha, it just means that they are accustomed to forcing stubborn animals to do what is required. Cattle can be incredibly difficult, so Corgis learned centuries ago that being bossy worked to get cattle to go where they should. This is why you need a firm, consistent approach to training your Corgi – the Corgi has to know that you are in charge. Your dog also needs to feel that you are capable of being in charge, and that means always acting like the leader.

Properly Greeting New People

Corgis have sensitive hearing, but that does not tend to make them particularly suspicious (just cautious). To ensure that your Corgi understands how to interact with others, you must socialize the puppy. It can be a lot of fun, so it isn't something most people avoid. (Who doesn't love meeting and playing with a lovable little dog?) The difficult part is finding the time to do it often enough to reinforce the positive behaviors and teach the puppy that the world is a fun place.

Greeting new people is usually a pretty easy task outside of the home, but can be a bit tricky when you are at home. The constant barking can frighten some visitors, and your Corgi will sense that. Thinking that it has the upper hand can end up making the Corgi incorrectly believe that the visitor is lower in the pack. Training your Corgi how to treat visitors may take awhile, but in the end, it is worth the effort as your Corgi becomes an enjoyable companion for you and anyone who visits.

Behavior around Other Dogs

Corgis are incredibly agreeable dogs. They do not need to be alpha, but they can believe that they know what is best for everyone. If you have an older dog, most Corgis will be able to peacefully work out who is alpha and who isn't without too many problems. Since Corgis hate to be alone, it is probably better to have another dog if you are absent from the home for hours every day.

Photo Courtesy of
Tammie Songer

CHAPTER 10

Being a Puppy Parent

Puppies are a lot of fun. They bring a whole new perspective to the world that people simply do not see without a puppy's guidance. At the same time, they can be difficult and destructive in a way that is both cute and frustrating.

When it comes to Corgis, this relationship is compounded by the fact that they are willful, intelligent, and individualistic, while also being incredibly affectionate and personable. If they sense any hesitation, they are smart enough to know how to exploit it. Like every other intelligent working dog, they will learn that they can manipulate you and the best ways to do it.

When properly trained, Corgis are incredible companions. It just takes a lot of work in those early days to ensure they learn the right habits.

Staying Consistently Firm

Photo Courtesy of
Gayla Miller

When it comes to training a Corgi, you must be firm and consistent. Over the course of its life, your Corgi is going to try to get away with misbehavior, not out of rebellion, but just to see if it can. It is one of the main reasons why you really cannot make exceptions to the rules, not even while it is still a puppy.

If you get accustomed to making exceptions because the puppy is adorable, you are not going to succeed in training your Corgi. Those cute little fox-like faces hide an incredibly sharp mind that will notice and remember an action that allowed them to get their way. Remember, they are intelligent and stubborn. You must be unyielding with your puppy if you want a well-behaved dog.

Your dog does not mean any harm and certainly is not trying to be rebellious. Corgis simply like to have things their own way, and they are generally clever enough to get it. However, it could mean that your dog does not respect you. That is why it is so important to be consistent and firm. Your dog has to know that you are the alpha of the pack at all times.

Puppy Gnawing and What to Watch

Puppies gnaw. At first, they are teething and it feels good to sink their teeth into something. Later, they do it as part of their learning and socialization. Corgis are one of the breeds that you must be particularly careful with because they have a tendency to be destructive when they are bored. Gnawing on things is part of a habit.

For the first few months after your puppy comes home, you should keep the pup secured in a place where there are only a few things to chew. You also need to make sure there is not a way for your puppy to escape. That means making sure there is no furniture or moveable objects that can be moved or knocked around and jumped up on. They start problem solving remarkably early, and while they are not prone to knocking down gates and boundaries, they are not averse to finding ways around them.

Photo Courtesy of Tammie Songer

When your puppy is not in the enclosed space, you must keep an eye on it at all times. Just like when you are taking care of an infant or toddler, once you turn to look away, that puppy is going to be getting into things it shouldn't be getting into. If you do not have time to keep an eye on your Corgi, keep it in a place where there is not much to chew on (besides the things you don't mind the puppy chewing).

You can keep toys and chewing toys around your puppy at all times, particularly in the Corgi's designated area. This helps the puppy learn what is appropriate to chew. Once it is time to come out and play, your Corgi will learn what not to chew, which is why you must keep your focus on the puppy. Over time, your dog will learn what is acceptable to use as a chew toy.

Puppy Nipping and What to Teach

In addition to gnawing, Corgis nip, particularly around young children. Teaching them not to do this goes against the instincts that have been bred into them over centuries, but it is not impossible. It is essential that you keep an eye on your puppy. At the first sign that the dog is nipping, you must step in and let the Corgi know that that is not acceptable. Usually there will be barking before the nipping starts. If you notice your puppy getting excited, try to calm it down before the nipping begins.

The puppy needs to learn that playing is acceptable, so do not dissuade the play, just the nipping. As long as the puppy is peaceful during play, you can enjoy playing.

You will also need to expose your puppy to other people to ensure the Corgi understands that the interaction needs to be consistent, no matter who is around. If you have children, you will need to make sure that the children understand that they can only play with the puppy when there is an adult around. Older kids should understand how to manage nipping.

Barking, Barking, and More Barking

Photo Courtesy of Susan Dale

It is nearly a guarantee that your Corgi is going to bark. While it is possible to train them to be quieter, the success rates vary.

If your puppy barks at you when you are doing something, simply ignore it. The barking is a way to force you to pay attention and include the puppy in your activities. If you aren't doing something that can include the puppy, it needs to learn that barking is not going to be effective. If your Corgi stops barking, give it a few moments to make sure the barking does not begin again, and then you can include it if possible. Your Corgi is smart and will quickly understand that being included means being there, and not barking.

There are a few other tricks, but that is one of the most basic training tips that you can start as soon as you get home with your puppy. This is the best way to start training your dog not to bark all of the time.

Destructive Behavior

Destructive behavior is a concern for all puppy parents, but this is particularly true for those who have intelligent working dogs as those dogs have a lot of energy and get bored very easily. Being destructive is their way of letting you know that they need to be entertained or employed in a task.

Inside

Corgis can actually destroy things that you would never expect them to because they are excellent problem solvers. If you think that the toys and writing implements on the coffee table are safe simply because it is over the puppy's head, you will find that the puppy can find a way to get to them anyway.

When it comes to Corgis, you have to do two things.

- Train them not to be destructive.
- Ensure that they cannot reach anything you don't want them to destroy/eat.

Toys can help, but usually not for long because your puppy will get bored with a new present just as fast as a toddler does. No toy is going to occupy a Corgi's attention for more than a few minutes, and then the pup is going to be off looking for something more interesting to do.

To keep your puppy and belongings safe, you must keep the Corgi locked up when you cannot focus on the puppy's activities.

Outside

Moving outside is not any less likely to curb your puppy's destructive tendencies, it will just take a little longer to get bored since there are so many smells. As soon as your puppy feels comfortable and bored, the chewing and destruction will begin.

Just like the precautions that you have to take inside, you have to make sure there is no way for the puppy to find a way to climb over your fence. Given their size, you also need to make sure the fence reaches the ground and there are no gaps where a Corgi can slip through to the outside. You will not be able to leave your puppy alone outside, and you will only be able to be marginally distracted while the puppy is exploring. Since a Corgi has such a small stature, once your puppy gets into something, it is going to be very difficult for you to find the puppy.

Plan to interact with your Corgi for the first few months while outside. This will make it easier to keep the puppy safe and your stuff (including plants) from being demolished.

Managing the Behavior

Given their high intellect and energy, the best preventative for destructive behavior is to always be attentive to the puppy and to make sure it gets enough exercise to minimize the tendencies. Corgis are a lot of fun to be with, so it really is not much of a chore to play with and walk your Corgi enough to tire it out.

If you are a constant companion and alpha personality, that ensures that your puppy learns to listen to and respect you.

During the early stages of the puppy's life you need to spend a lot of time keeping the puppy active so it will be too tired to misbehave. You also need to start training as early as possible so that by the time the Corgi's stamina improves, the training is enough to keep it in check.

Photo Courtesy of Liza Gagne

Play Time!

Playtime is awesome for you and for your puppy. Corgis just want to be with their pack having a good time, and you are giving it everything it needs to stay out of trouble. (Not to mention they are so incredibly cute as puppies that it is hardly a chore to play with them until they are too tired to do much.)

Make time in the schedule for regular playtime. No matter how busy you are, this is something that you need to do several times a day to properly train your Corgi. They do not like to be alone, and this is the period of time when they really start to understand the rules and boundaries. You can train your dog over the course of its entire life, but what you teach now will have a huge effect on how well you can train it as it matures and afterward. Remember, this is the foundation for all later training.

Start teaching the puppy tricks as early as possible too. This not only keeps your Corgi's mind working, it can help you bond. It is a remarkably enjoyable way to engage the Corgi in physical and mental stimulation that will reduce the tendency to chew and destroy everything nearby.

Corgis love to be with you, and they want to impress you with what they can do. Being taken out to explore and be active is the pinnacle of the best life to a Corgi. Playing with your puppy provides a safe and fun environment to learn how to behave. Your dedication now will equate to an adorable, loving, loyal companion for a long time.

*Photo Courtesy of
Caitlin Cassity*

CHAPTER 11

Living with Other Dogs

Both types of Welsh Corgis are likely to get along great with your other dogs, especially if you start with a puppy. As the kind of dog that hates to be alone, your Corgi will be much happier having another dog around the home while you are gone.

It may take them a couple of days to figure out who is boss of the dogs, but in most instances you won't have to worry about it too much. Corgis are clever enough to get their way even if the other dog or dogs believe they are on top.

Introducing Your New Puppy

Photo Courtesy of Janet Maddox

The introductions need to start in a neutral place because your dog may feel territorial. Neutral ground will make your dog feel more at ease with the new puppy since the new Corgi is not invading your dog's space. It doesn't matter what breed the puppy is--this is always true when introducing a new dog to your home.

As your puppy and dog (or dogs) begin to feel comfortable around each other, you can start to make your way back home. When they all enter the home together, there will already be some familiarity between your puppy and the rest of your pack.

This sense of familiarity is not an instant bond. You need to keep the puppy and your other dogs separated when you are not around. The puppy should have some personal space where only it can rest. This was part of the initial prep work, so by the time your puppy comes into the home, this area should already be established.

There should be nothing in the puppy's area that belongs to your other dogs. This can create unnecessary tension and problems that are not likely to be resolved peacefully. Your Corgi will want to chew everything, and the concept of possession doesn't really mean anything to it quite yet. However, your current dog will see it as a challenge to its place, and may act accordingly. This is also true when your puppy is outside of its own designated area. You need to make sure there is nothing that belongs to your other dog within the puppy's reach. All you have to do is store the other dog's toys when it is time for the puppy to play.

Feeding time for different pets should take place in different locations in your home. Food is one of the biggest causes of jealousy, and you do not want there to be that kind of unnecessary tension between your puppy and your current pets. It may be possible to move the bowls closer together later to make feeding time more convenient, but in the beginning you should keep them separated.

Dogs get jealous when they see their people giving attention to other dogs, even puppies. Be prepared for this when you bring home the puppy. You will need to make sure your dog continues to get one-on-one time with you so that it does not feel like the puppy is replacing it. Make sure you already have established rules and schedules so that you can give your dog enough attention on a daily basis. You will need to be firm and consistent with both your puppy and your dog.

One of the biggest benefits of having a dog is that your dog is very likely to automatically start to scold your puppy. Your dog is not going to feel the same fit of adoration that you do when looking at the puppy, making your dog a great mentor and teacher for the Corgi puppy. While you cannot rely on the dog to be the primary trainer of your Corgi, it will help the puppy understand where it is in the pack and that certain behaviors are not acceptable. You can let your dog do some scolding and reprimanding, but do make sure that the puppy is not being harmed. Thinking of your dog as a babysitter can help you establish the right balance in how the dog and puppy interact.

If your dog does not assume a this role, that is also alright. You don't want to try to force a role on your dog with the new puppy. The canines will figure it out if you just give them time and supervise them until their relationship is established.

Working Dog Mentality

There is a distinct mentality that all working dogs have, even the charming little Corgi. They are accustomed to being the one in charge

Photo Courtesy of Betsy Ellsworth

when around other animals, and this may affect how they feel about your other pets. That trait is going to come out in your puppy at some point, and the nipping and barking will be noticeable. The puppy is not trying to misbehave–its breeding tells it that this is acceptable (and necessary) behavior.

As the human, your role is to make sure that you know which dog is established as the dominant canine. You need to know because you will need to address your furry family members based on the order they set.

As your Corgi puppy grows and starts to challenge your dog, you need to be aware of the potentially changing dynamic. It is possible that your youngest canine will end up being the dominant dog in the home (this is entirely likely if your other dog is a spaniel or another mellow breed).

Once you know who the alpha is, you will need to greet the alpha dog first, leash the alpha first, and feed the alpha first. This can help reduce fights and the feeling that your older dog is being undermined if it is the dominant dog.

You can also use this method to train your Corgi puppy that the older dog is the alpha. By always acknowledging the dog first, you are letting the puppy know that the older dog is higher up in the pack. As the puppy ages this may change, but it may also be imprinted on the puppy's mind. Some Corgis will easily accept this, so that you can avoid the entire ordeal of establishing an alpha dog.

Biting, Fighting, and Puppy Anger Management

Puppies are a handful for many reasons, but this can be one of the most challenging problems of dealing with a young dog. Corgis are known for being pretty even-tempered, but you do have to watch for aggression when the puppy is young. There will be times when the puppy is not happy, and the result may be nipping and lashing out at your other dog. This is extremely likely when your Corgi puppy reaches adult size.

Being firm and consistent is the only way to deal with this problem.

An untrained Corgi can actually be a pretty monstrous dog because it has not been taught that it cannot force others to do things a certain way.

You do need to spend a lot of time with the puppy so that you can understand when it is being playful and when it is upset. When you spot aggressive behavior (not just play), you have to immediately step in and train your Corgi that that is unacceptable behavior.

Starting training at a very early stage can help you see when your puppy is being playful, and when the behavior goes a little further than playful.

Raising Multiple Puppies at Once

Photo Courtesy of Jessi Hall

Raising one puppy is nearly a full-time job, but there are some who take on raising two at a time. If you want to raise two Corgi puppies at the same time, you are definitely in for a challenge. These dogs are nobody's fool, and when they put their heads together, you are going to have a hard time outsmarting them. You are going to have to really work to get them to behave the way you want them to once they reach maturity.

One of the first things you will notice is that your personal life disappears. You are going to be tending to your puppies for the majority of your day. This is absolutely essential if you do not want to have twice the destruction in your home.

First, you have to spend time with both of them together, and you will also have to give them each alone time. They are not the same dog, so you cannot treat them that way. Each puppy will have different strengths and weaknesses. Spending time with them together is easy, but you must take time with them on their own as well. It will be a challenge, especially when one whines as you play with the other. One of the best ways to deal with this is to have someone else play with the other puppy, then switch. This keeps both puppies happily occupied so that they don't get jealous.

Just as your puppy is likely to fight with an older dog, the Corgi puppies are almost certainly going to start fighting with each other when they are between three and six months old. They are establishing who is the dominant dog, and that is fine. You just need to make sure they understand that you are the alpha of the pack so that they do not start to question your authority over them.

Just as you need to minimize the puppies' distractions (and they will be their own worst distractions), you have to minimize your own. If you are preparing their food, you need to stay focused on that until the puppies are eating. If you are getting ready for a walk, as soon as you get the leashes on, get out the door. The puppies are watching and learning, so show them how to stay focused and follow through. If you do not, you have no one to blame but yourself when they start to get rowdy and unmanageable. After all, you got them excited about eating or walking, only to leave them waiting. Dogs do not understand the concept of patience, but with all of that excitement now pent up and ready to burst, you are going to be the one who suffers for failing to follow through with the activity.

Remember, their misbehavior is really a reflection of how you have trained them. If you constantly require them to focus during training, but you fail to focus on tasks with them, both of your puppies are going to notice. Be consistent and focused to avoid many unnecessary issues with your puppies.

If you find you cannot decide if you want a Pembroke or a Cardigan Welsh Corgi, you can get one of each. It is very likely you will find that the dogs end up being pretty similar, highlighting how training, environment, and attention play a large role in how the puppy grows up. Or you may find that your two dogs have very different and distinct personalities. It is certainly an interesting experiment that can give you something to watch for years. And it will give you a much better understanding of the breed.

CHAPTER 12

Training Your Welsh Corgi Puppy

Corgis can understand far more than the average dog, and they are always looking for ways to use that to their advantage. Their energy is high for such a compact dog, but not unmanageably so. But that brain of theirs can get them into some pretty hot water if you don't give them ways to keep from getting bored.

Photo Courtesy of Cherie Doyle

When you are dealing with smart, energetic puppies, there are some things that you absolutely must do, and then there are things you should do. Either way, training is a long-term commitment with a Corgi because once you set the rules there is really no way you can deviate. Any exception to a rule is likely to be used against you later. Corgis are not rebellious, they are just unbelievably intelligent and don't like being told no. However, with the right training, they will respect your "no" rather than disappoint the alpha.

Firm AND Consistent

Unless you take a firm and consistent approach with your Corgi, you are not going to be successful in training. Exceptions and leniency are seen as you relinquishing your position, or indicate that there is room for the Corgi to make decisions. Your Corgi is going to take that as the template for how to get its own way going forward.

Staying consistent and firm is going to be difficult. You will be tired or have a rough day, but you have to keep it up, no matter how cute your puppy is being or how much you just want to sit and cuddle instead of doing the regular training work.

Training is a way to teach your puppy, and all working dogs require that you stay focused, take a consistent approach, and remain firm when enforcing the training. Flexibility comes much later when the dog understands what all of the rules are.

Right now, you are teaching your puppy its place in the pack. There should not be any question that you are the alpha dog of the pack. While Corgis don't have to be the alpha, they do like to have a say. If it is not clear that you are a firm alpha, they are going to try to work the situation in a way that will give them more of a say in how the house is run.

One thing to keep in mind is that dogs are not comfortable if the pack hierarchy is not well-defined. They require structure and a place to be comfortable. If you fail to be consistent and firm, that is a signal that the structure is undefined. Your Corgi is going to want to define the positions. Corgis have no problem not being the alpha, but they do need to know who is. They also need to know their place to avoid getting anxious and stressed.

Photo Courtesy of Gayla Miller

Gain Their Respect Early

Dogs operate on a basis of respect. Without respect, they are not going to listen to you.

Remember that fear and respect are not the same thing. You want your dog to love you, not fear you.

Getting your Corgi to respect you is actually relatively easy. As long as you are firm and consistent, you Corgi is going to feel comfortable. That also means you need to stay focused. If you are constantly trying to multi-task and fail to complete what you are doing, you are not going to get your dog's respect (of course, that means tasks related to your Corgi – it is not going to know whether you complete non-dog-related tasks).

One of the best ways to get a Corgi's respect is through positive interaction, especially positive reinforcement. By spending time with your puppy, you are building a healthy relationship and showing the puppy where it falls in the pack order. Ultimately, Corgis just want to be with you having a good time. As long as you are firm and consistent, your Corgi is going to respect you.

Operant Conditioning Basics

Operant conditioning is a more scientific term for actions and consequences. What you have to do is provide your Corgi puppy with the right consequences for each behavior.

With a working dog, the best way to use operant conditioning is through positive reinforcement. This type of training is more effective with working dogs because they want to please their people. They want to work with you and fulfill their tasks. Knowing that they are doing something right does a lot more to encourage their behavior than knowing when they do something wrong. With so much energy, they will be able to keep trying until they get it right.

There are two types of reinforcements for operant conditioning:
- Primary reinforcements
- Secondary reinforcements

You will use both during your Corgi's training.

Primary Reinforcements

A primary reinforcement gives your dog something that it needs to survive, like food or social interaction. Both of these are incredibly effective reinforcements for Corgis – they love treats and spending time with you. That is exactly what makes these rewards so effective during training.

Initially, you will rely on primary reinforcements because you do not have to teach your Corgi to enjoy them. However, you have to keep a balance. Mealtime and playtime should never be denied to your Corgi, no matter how poorly your dog performs. These things are essential to living, and you will have to give them – that is not negotiable. It is things like treats and extra playtime that are used to reinforce good behavior.

Err on the side of providing too much attention and affection over too many treats. With their small stature, Corgis need to keep a well-balanced diet to be healthy. If you rely on treats instead of attention, you are setting up yourself and your pup for serious problems later.

Secondary Reinforcements

You have probably used repetition to get good at your hobbies, sports, and other physical activities – this is secondary reinforcement. Without a doubt, Pavlov's experiment with dogs is the most recogniz-

Photo Courtesy of
Jessi Hall

able example of secondary reinforcement. Using a bell, Pavlov taught the dogs that when the bell rang it meant it was time to eat. The test dogs began to associate the ringing of a bell with meal time. They were conditioned to associate something unrelated with a primary reinforcement. You can see this in your home when you use a can opener. If you have any cats or dogs, they probably come running as soon as the can opener starts going.

Secondary reinforcements work because your Corgi will associate the trigger with something that is required. This makes your puppy more likely to do as you tell it to do. Dogs who are taught to sit using a treat only will automatically react by sitting down when you have a treat in your hand. They won't even wait for you to tell them to sit. They know that sitting means more food, so they automatically do it once you make that association. Of course, this is not the proper training because they need to learn to sit when you say sit, not when you have a treat. That is the real challenge.

Fortunately, it is relatively easy to train a Corgi with the right trigger because they are incredibly intelligent. While they love food, you can show them that the trigger is the word, not the food. They will get it much faster than most other types of dogs.

Photo Courtesy of
Jessica Burleski

You can also use toys and attention as a way of getting your Corgi puppy to do the right thing. If you have a regular schedule and you are willing to change it a little to give your puppy a little extra attention for doing something right, that will be just as effective as a treat because they love attention. You can take the pup on an extra walk, spend a little more time playing with a favorite toy, or take some time to cuddle with the puppy.

Sometimes punishment is required too, but you need to be very careful about how you do it. Trying to punish a Corgi can be tricky, but denying your Corgi your attention can work very well. Simply put your puppy in a penned-off area where the Corgi can see you but cannot interact with you. The little guy will whine and whimper to let you know that it wants out. Don't give in because this is the punishment. Just ignore your puppy so that the Corgi learns not to misbehave.

Punishments must happen right after the undesired behavior. If your Corgi chews something up and you don't find out for several hours, it is too late to punish the puppy. The same is true for rewards. To reinforce behavior, the reward or punishment must be almost immediate. When you praise or punish your puppy, make sure you keep eye contact. You can also take the puppy by the scruff of the neck to ensure you keep eye contact. You won't need to do that when you are praising your pooch because it will automatically keep eye contact. Corgis love to hear about what they did right and love to hear your praise.

Why Food Is a Bad Reinforcement Tool

With the small stature of a Corgi, food is not something you should use often. It does not take much for a Corgi to gain too much weight. With affection and attention being such successful motivators, it is best to use them as much as possible instead of getting your Corgi accustomed to treats for rewards. Use them sparingly.

Another reason to use treats sparingly is because you don't want your puppy to respond to you primarily when you have food. If your Corgi associates training with treats, you may have a difficult time training your Corgi to listen to you without them.

Treats can be used in the early stages when your puppy's metabolism is high and it has not been conditioned to respond to secondary reinforcement. This will give you something to help your puppy learn to focus as you train it to understand other incentives. It should not take too long before you can start transitioning. Treats are also the best way of training certain types of behavior, such as rolling over. Your puppy will automatically follow the treat, making it easy for it to understand what you mean.

Treats are also best for the beginning commands (sit, stay, and leave it). Your dog does not understand words yet, and will quickly make the connection between what you are saying and why the treat is being offered. Leave it is very difficult to teach without treats because there is no incentive to drop something if your puppy really wants the object already in its mouth. Treats are something that will make the puppy drop whatever it has as its attention and desire focus on the food.

Small Steps to Success

For the first few weeks and months, your puppy is not going to understand what you are doing as you try to train it where to use the bathroom. You need to realize that you will have to start slow and build up a daily routine. Your puppy is in a new place and that will be a distraction until the place is familiar. Once the place is less exciting, the puppy will be able to focus on training without as many distractions.

Training really does need to begin as soon as you bring your puppy home. As your puppy gets familiar with the surroundings you can teach it to go into the kennel. Learning to go into the crate on command has some very obvious benefits, especially when you need to leave and you don't feel like fighting with the puppy. It is also a great way to introduce the puppy to treats as a reward so that the rest of the training runs a little smoother.

You have to start small. Once your Corgi gets the hang of the rewards system, training will begin to be much easier and faster.

Why Trainers Aren't Always Necessary

Corgis love to please their people. When they misbehave, it is almost always out of boredom. This is something you can easily control if you are not gone for large chunks of the day. If you will be gone for a long time (six or more hours), the best way to keep Corgi puppies from being destructive is to keep them in their crates when you are gone. If you have older dogs, they are a great way to keep Corgis in check and entertained. While you will have to use the crate in the beginning, even with a dog, over time, the older dog or dogs can start helping the pup to spend time out of the crate. This should be done in small increments though. You don't let the puppy stay out of the crate for a full day. If you have a couple of errands to do and will be back in about thirty minutes or so, that should be a good start with the older dog in charge.

Apart from you and an older dog, Corgis really don't need any special trainers. If you do not have the time to do the training yourself, you should consider a trainer. However, if you are going to get a Corgi puppy, it is much better to make sure you have time to do the training. Training builds bonds and respect that are invaluable to succeeding if you want to do more advanced training.

If you have never trained a puppy, a class can be incredibly helpful to show you how it is done. However, it really is not necessary to have your own trainer to help. Your Corgi wants time with you and wants to make you happy – that gives you a distinct advantage when it comes to training.

Photo Courtesy of Kandace Wilkens

CHAPTER 13

Basic Commands

There are so many things you can train a Corgi to do, from fetch to feats of agility, and that training all starts with a few simple commands. With these commands, your puppy will learn not only to do the most basic and necessary actions, but will also learn how to learn. Once your puppy has these commands down, the possibilities are endless.

Why Size and Personality Make Them Ideal Companions

Training is essential for Corgis. They are incredibly intelligent, and that means they need to be trained in order to be good companions. When properly trained, they can be one of the best companions because they can travel with you anywhere you go. If a Corgi is well trained, the people around you will enjoy having the dog around too because Corgis are famously fun and energetic. They tend to love everyone and want to play. Since they can go with you virtually anywhere, training will quickly pay off as you and your best friend share some of the most memorable adventures. If your Corgi is not trained, it will be much harder to take your canine places because it is likely to bark too much and destroy things everywhere you go.

Picking the Right Reward

One of the most interesting aspects of having a Corgi is determining the right reward. You want to keep the treats to a minimum, but that should be fine with a Corgi since there are so many other things that can motivate them. Treats may be a good starting point, but you will need to quickly switch to something that is a secondary reinforcer. Praise, additional play time, and extra petting are all fantastic rewards for Corgis since they care about how you feel and react.

If you begin to gain your Corgi's respect, that can also be used to help train your dog. The respect won't be there when you begin the basic commands, but after a few weeks, you will start to see how it provides your Corgi the motivation to do what you ask. At the end of each session, give your puppy extra attention or a nice walk to demonstrate how pleased you are with the progress that has been made.

Successful Training

Training is about learning the commands. If your Corgi learns to respond only to the rewards (like the dog that sits as soon as you have a treat in your hand), the training was not successful.

Photo Courtesy of
Kandace Wilkens

Respect is generally the key in being a successful trainer. As you and your Corgi work together, your dog will come to respect you (so long as you remain consistent and firm). Do not expect respect in the early days of training because your relationship with your puppy hasn't developed enough yet and it is too young to understand. Fortunately, that Corgi intelligence will start to show early on, making it easy to see when your puppy is starting to respond to your reaction instead of just the reward. This is the time when you can start switching to rewards that are fun instead of those that center around treats and food.

Even in the beginning, you need to make handling and petting part of the reward. Soon your Corgi will begin to understand that treats and petting are both rewards. This will make it easier to switch from treats to a more attention-based reward system. Associating handling and petting as being enjoyable will also encourage your puppy to look at playtime as a great reward. No matter how much it loves to eat, being entertained and playing with you will be a welcome reward since it means the puppy is not alone or bored.

Basic Commands

Photo Courtesy of Jessica Burleski

For Corgis, there are five basic commands that you must teach, and one more that you will probably want to start training your puppy to understand. These commands are the basis for a happy and enjoyable relationship as your Corgi learns how to behave. By the time it learns these commands, the purpose of training will be clear to your Corgi. That will make it much easier to teach more complex concepts.

You should teach these commands in the order they are listed. Sit is a basic command, and something dogs already do; they just have to learn to do it on command. Teaching leave it and how to bark less are both difficult commands that go against your Corgi's instincts and desires. They are going to take longer than the rest, so you want to have the necessary foundation already in place to increase your odds of success.

Here are some basic guidelines to follow during training.

- Everyone in the home should be a part of the Corgi's training because it needs to learn to listen to everyone, not just one or two people.
- To get started, select an area where you and your puppy have no distractions, including noise. Leave your phone and other devices out of range so that you keep your attention on the puppy.
- Stay happy and excited about the training. Your puppy will pick up on your enthusiasm, and will focus better because of it.
- Start to teach sit when you puppy is around eight weeks old.
- Be consistent as you teach.
- Bring a special treat to the first few training sessions, such as chicken or cheese.

Once you are prepared, you can get started working and bonding with your cute little Corgi.

Sit

Once you settle into your quiet training location with the special treat, begin the training. It is relatively easy to teach this command. Wait until your puppy starts to sit down and say sit at the same time. If your puppy finishes sitting down, start to praise it. Naturally, this will make your puppy incredibly excited and wiggly, so it may take awhile before it will want to sit again. When the time comes and the puppy starts to sit again, repeat the process.

It is going to take more than a couple of sessions for the puppy to fully connect your words with its actions. In fact, it could take a little over a week to get it. Corgis are intelligent, but at this age there is still so much to learn that the puppy will have a hard time focusing. Commands are something completely new. However, once your puppy understands your intention and masters sit, the other commands will be easier to teach.

Once your puppy has demonstrated mastery over *sit*, it is time to start teaching *down*.

Down

Repeat the same process to teach this one as you did for *sit*. Wait until the puppy starts to lie down, then say the word. If the Corgi finishes the action, offer your chosen reward.

It will likely take a little less time to teach this one after you start.

Wait until you puppy has mastered *down* before moving on to *stay*.

Stay

This command is going to be more difficult since it isn't something that your puppy does naturally. Be prepared for it to take a bit longer to train on this one. It is also important that your dog will consistently sit and lie down on command before you start to teach *stay*.

Choose whether to use the *sit* or *down* command to get started, then be consistent. Once your dog understands stay for either sit or down, you can train it to stay in the other position. Just make sure the first position is mastered before trying the second.

Give your puppy either the sit or *down* command. As you do this, place your hand in front of the puppy's face. Wait until the puppy stops trying to lick you before you continue.

When the puppy settles down, take a step away. If your puppy is not moving, say stay and give the puppy the treat and some praise for staying.

Giving the reward to your puppy indicates that the command is over, but the puppy also has to learn to stay until you say it is okay to leave the spot. Once you give the okay to move, do not give treats. *Come* should not be used as the okay word as it is a command used for something else.

Repeat the steps, taking more steps further away from the puppy after a successful command.

Once your puppy understands *stay* when you move away, start training to *stay* even if you are not moving. Extend the amount of time required for the puppy to stay in one spot until it understands that *stay* ends with the okay command.

When you feel that your puppy has *stay* mastered, start to train the puppy to *come.*

Come

This is the last in the series of commands as you cannot teach this one until the puppy has learned the previous commands.

Before you start, decide if you want to use *come* or *come here* for the command. You will need to be consistent in the words you use, so make sure you plan it so that you (and other family members) will intentionally use the right command every time.

Leash the puppy.

Tell the puppy to *stay*. Move away from the puppy.

Say the command you will use for *come* and give a gentle tug on the leash toward you. As long as you did not use the term to indicate that the

*Photo Courtesy of
Jessi Hall*

stay command was done, your puppy will begin to understand the purpose of your new command. If you used the term to indicate the end of stay, it will confuse your puppy because it will associate the command with being able to move freely.

Repeat these steps, building a larger distance between you and the puppy. Once the puppy seems to get it, remove the leash and start again at a close distance. If your puppy does not seem to understand the command, give some visual clues about what you want. For example, you can pat your leg or snap your fingers. As soon as your puppy comes to you, offer a reward.

Leave It

This is going to be one of the most difficult commands you will teach your puppy because it goes against both the Corgi's instincts and its interests. Your puppy wants to keep whatever it has, so you are going to have to offer something better. It is essential to teach it early, though, as your Corgi is going to be very destructive in the early days. You want to get the trigger in place to convince the puppy to drop things.

You may need to start teaching this outside of the training area since it has a different starting point.

Start when you have time to dedicate to the lesson. You have to wait until the puppy has something in its mouth to drop. Toys are usually best. Offer the puppy a special treat. As the Corgi drops the toy, say *leave it*, and hand over the treat.

This is going to be one of those rare times when you must use a food treat because your puppy needs something convincing to make it decide to drop the toy. For now, your puppy needs the incentive of something more tempting than what it already has to learn the command.

This will be one of the two commands that will take the longest to teach (*quiet* being the other). Be prepared to be patient with your pup. Once your puppy gets it, start to teach *leave it* with food. This is incredibly important to do because it could save your Corgi's life. It is likely to lunge at things that look like food when you are out for a walk, and being so low to the ground, it is probably going to see a lot of food-like things long before you do. This command teaches it to drop whatever it is munching before ingesting it.

Quiet

In the beginning, you can also use treats sparingly to reinforce *quiet*. If your puppy is barking for no apparent reason, tell the puppy to be quiet and place a treat in front of it. It is almost guaranteed that the dog will fall silent to sniff the treat, in which case, say *good dog* or *good quiet*. It will not take too long for your puppy to understand that *quiet* means no barking. However, it may take a while for your puppy to learn to fight the urge to bark. Be patient with your puppy because it is difficult to stop doing something that it does naturally. How long did it take you to learn to get up early in the morning or to go to bed at a certain time? It is similar for a Corgi to learn not to bark.

Where to Go from Here

These are all the commands that you are likely to truly need with your Corgi. However, if you want your Corgi to do tricks, you can pretty much go anywhere from here. These commands are the foundation of training, and Corgis are capable of learning so much more. Just make sure that the tricks that you teach are not too stressful for your puppy. As your puppy ages, you can start teaching tricks that highlight its agility. *Fetch* and other interactive tricks will be ideal because your Corgi will want to do them.

CHAPTER 14

Nutrition

Just as your own nutrition is important, what your Corgi eats plays a large role in how healthy and energetic it will be. With Corgis, you need to be particularly careful because they are so agile and clever. You must make sure your Corgi cannot get into food that you do not intend for the dog to eat. That means making sure you do not leave food where your Corgi can get it (and that is a lot more places than you may think).

While you are making sure it doesn't eat things it shouldn't, you also have to make sure your Corgi gets a balanced diet. This ensures that it can continue to be happy and energetic well into its golden years.

*Photo Courtesy of
Liza Gagne*

Why a Healthy Diet is Important

Corgis are a relatively high-energy breed (especially for their size). Their small stature may make it easier to exercise them than many of the larger breed working dogs, but they still require a lot more activity than the average dog. As busy as most people are, it may be difficult to get out and exercise your Corgi every day. A healthy, well-balanced diet is essential to ensuring your canine does not start putting on extra weight which will be very detrimental to its health.

You must be aware of your Corgi's eating habits and ensure that the food that it consumes is part of a balanced diet (with the occasional treat). Pay attention to the calorie count of the food you purchase or make, and ensure that all of the most important vitamins and nutrients are part of your Corgi's regular diet.

Commercial Food

Commercial dog food is incredibly flawed. As an entirely processed food, it is not going to be as healthy for your Corgi as food you make yourself. Your dog will not be able to process all of the nutrients in commercial dog food either. However, many people do not have adequate time to prepare good food even for themselves – cooking for your dog too may seem like an impossible addition to your day.

If you read the label and purchase one of the premium commercial dog foods, you can give your Corgi food that more closely aligns with its needs. You can add a few extras to your dog's daily commercial diet to supplement any nutrients that you think are missing. A little bit of home-cooked food every day will also be an incredibly welcome addition for your Corgi.

Preparing Your Food Naturally at Home

Home-cooked food may take you an extra five to ten minutes a day, but ultimately it is worth it. You can even make it from the same ingredients you use while you are working on your own food. Though your Corgi's dietary needs are different from yours, you can mix in some of your food with your Corgi's food (keeping in mind not to add the foods that are potentially deadly to your dog – review Chapter 5 for the list of what not to give your Corgi).

While you don't want to feed your dog before you eat (the alpha of a pack always eats first), you can leave the food on the counter or on the

Photo Courtesy of
Dawn Blanchard

stove to simmer, then feed your pup when you are done. The best home-cooked meals need to be planned so that you know your dog is getting the right nutrients.

Typically, 50 percent of your dog's food should be animal protein, such as oily fish, poultry, and organ meats. A quarter of the food should contain complex carbohydrates, and the remaining quarter should be vegetables and fruits. Pumpkin, apples, bananas, and green beans are excellent foods for dogs that also have a smell that your Corgi is likely to love. They can also help your dog feel fuller faster so that it is less likely to overeat.

Puppy Food vs. People Food

If you plan to get (or already have) a Corgi puppy but know you will not have time to cook, make sure you pick up food that is specifically made for puppies. Do not feed the puppy people food thinking that it will be okay for now – because it won't be. Your Corgi will think that it should be getting food from your plate or the kitchen and is likely to later refuse to eat dog food. It is a terrible precedent to set when your dog is young.

It is best to make your puppy's food if you can. Its body has special needs as it grows, and the first few months are particularly critical. If you can make your puppy's food for the first year or so, then switch to commercial dog food, that will be very beneficial to your Corgi. It will also be a bit kinder on your wallet.

Dieting, Exercise, and Obesity

Dogs don't diet the way people do. You have to establish a regular eating schedule and stick to it. If you make treats and snacks a regular part of your Corgi's diet, you better believe your Corgi will expect them every day. It is a terrible habit to get into with any dog, but it is particularly dangerous for Corgis.

Instead of giving your canine treats, spend a little more time showing affection. When you sit down to watch TV, let your Corgi sit beside you (if you have a "no dogs on the couch" policy, sit on the floor with your Corgi). Go outside and throw a ball for your Corgi. Take an extra walk.

Your Corgi needs a balanced diet and frequent exercise. This is not only healthier for your Corgi, it is better for you too. Without enough exercise, your dog will be inclined to become obese, and that will be a serious problem later in life. Get accustomed to exercise and play as a reward system instead of treats. This ends up being a much better deal for both of you.

Warning about Overfeeding and the Right Caloric Requirement

You need to be very careful of your Corgi's weight, particularly once your puppy becomes an adult. Corgis love to eat, and you will be tempted to give in and give your dog food from time to time. However, this is not a reward for your Corgi – it's a hazard. It is best to keep your dog on a healthy diet.

You can check your Corgi's weight regularly to ensure that it has not gotten out of control. Because Corgis are small, you can use your own scale to weigh them. Gently pick up your Corgi and step on the scale. Subtract your weight, and that is your Corgi's weight. Do be honest about your own weight though – no claiming that it is your dog's extra weight and not your own!

Counting calories can be time consuming, but you should have an idea of how many calories your dog has consumed every day.

Photo Courtesy of
Cindy Duwe

CHAPTER 15

Grooming – Productive Bonding

One of the things that people love about Corgis (apart from their fantastic personalities and willingness to try new adventures) is how easy it is to take care of their coats. Over centuries, their coats became essentially dirt resistant, making it incredibly easy to groom them.

However, they are prolific shedders. While their coat requires very little attention, if you don't want mounds of Corgi fur traversing your home, you will need to make regular grooming part of your routine.

Think of grooming as a way to bond with your Corgi. You will get to spend extra time petting and handling your dog, reinforcing your status as alpha and reducing your level of stress.

There are a few other grooming tips you should know to properly take care of your sweet little pup all the way through the golden years.

Managing Your Corgi's Coat

Brushing your Corgi can actually be a great way to bond with your dog and gives you dedicated time together. Your dog will love the regular attention, and you will enjoy the time to just be with your dog. Since Corgis are so small, you won't have to spend more than a few minutes on brushing.

Puppyhood

Puppies will take a bit longer to brush because they are not likely to sit still. They are going to want to play, nip, and generally do anything else. It's quite adorable, although if you brush weekly, it will mean putting more time aside than you may have initially thought you needed. You can brush when your puppy is too tired to cause trouble or use it as part of the training for being calm. Be careful not to encourage rambunctious behavior during brushing because it will be difficult to train your adult Corgi that this is not acceptable behavior.

*Photo Courtesy of
Betsy Ellsworth*

Adulthood

It is best to brush your Corgi at least once a week to keep the shedding to a minimum. During spring and summer when your Corgi is shedding more than usual, you may want to increase to three or four times a week.

You should only bathe your Corgi about once a quarter (or even twice a year). They have special oils in their fur that keep the dirt out, and if you bathe your Corgi often, it will remove these oils. Unless your Corgi rolls in something it shouldn't, just the occasional bath should be adequate to keep your loving pup clean.

Photo Courtesy of Elizabeth Schiavello

Bathing: Watch the Ears, Shampoos

Baths are not going to be a frequent chore, which is great considering your dog probably is not going to like it. Make sure you get a safe shampoo for your Corgi. However, no matter what kind of shampoo you get, do not let the shampoo get in your Corgi's ears.

You should take this time to check your Corgi's ears for infection, as well as making sure its ears are still dry after the bath. It will be a bit tricky, so be careful.

Should water get in your Corgi's ears, you will need to check them for several days afterward to make sure that the ears do not get infected.

Trimming the Nails

This is going to be the task that will probably cause you the most trouble, but if your Corgi respects you, it will not be too difficult to teach your dog to sit still for nail trimming.

You will probably need to cut the puppy's nails once a week. It will not be walking or running on hard surfaces as often, so its nails will not be worn down.

For adults, plan to check the nails monthly. If the nails are being naturally worn down (by walking on concrete and other hard surfaces outside), then you will not need to trim them.

Brushing Teeth

You should be brushing your Corgi's teeth about once a month, from puppyhood to the golden years. This not only helps keep your dog's teeth clean and healthy, it promotes fresher breath. If you notice that plaque and tartar are building up quickly, you can increase how often you brush your dog's teeth.

Cleaning Ears and Eyes

You will need to take extra care of your Corgi's ears. At least once a month, you should check your dog's ears for build-up of wax, infection, or other potential problems. Use a cotton ball with a cleaner that your vet approves to gently clean the ears. You should not be trying to go deep.

Never use a cotton swab on your Corgi's ears. You can do serious damage to the ear canal.

Corgis do not tend to have many problems with their eyes, but you should still check to make sure that your Corgi does not have a lot of dirt in them after an outdoor adventure. If it looks like dirt has gotten in your dog's eyes, you can use an eye wash approved by your vet. Usually, if your dog's fur is coated in dirt, then you should check to make sure the dirt and mud did not get in its eyes.

Photo Courtesy of
Cherie Doyle

CHAPTER 16

Basic Health Care

Corgis are well loved because of their small stature and great per-sonalities, but one of the things that makes them such success-ful working dogs is how sturdy, hardy, and healthy they are. As long as you take care of your Corgi, you will have a companion for many years to come. You do need to be careful with your Corgi though, because it is likely to fail to realize when it has sustained an injury. It is too focused on having adventures and enjoying time with you.

Beyond making sure your Corgi does not over-exert itself, you need to do some basic preventative care to make sure your dog does not have any easily preventable problems. Many of these treatments and con-cerns are universal in the canine world, so if you have other dogs, you probably already know about most of these tips. Take this chapter as a reminder that you need to keep it up with your Corgi (and make sure you add the treatments and monitoring into your budget).

Photo Courtesy of Elizabeth Schiavello

Fleas and Ticks

Corgis love to be active, and while you can get out often without going into areas that are likely to have fleas and ticks, it is always best to err on the side of caution and check your dog. If your Corgi loves going romping in high grass or in the woods, you definitely need to make sure there is no lapse in treatments.

Since you won't be bathing your Corgi often, you will need to check it over for ticks after being in the woods. Be sure to do your weekly brushing after going through the forest or places where your Corgi could pick up ticks. Comb through your Corgi's fur, looking for ticks in the fur and attached to the skin. Since you will be brushing your dog regularly, the bumps and other potential signs of ticks will be easier to spot. Also, since your Corgi is relatively small, it shouldn't take too long to go all the way through the process.

Fleas will be a little bit more difficult to notice. The best way to look for them is to conduct a routine check, such as when you do your weekly brushing. If you notice your Corgi scratching more than normal, you can start looking through its fur for fleas.

Even if you don't go into areas that are likely to have ticks, the Corgi's low position makes it likely that at least fleas are a constant threat since fleas can be in lawns and other manicured green spaces. If you find that your dog does have fleas, you may need to switch to a different flea preventative product.

If you prefer a more natural approach to managing fleas and ticks, you will need to set aside a few hours to research alternatives. You

Photo Courtesy of
Cherie Doyle

should not increase the number of baths your Corgi takes, so you will need to make sure that regular washing is not a part of any natural remedy you select. You also need to verify that the product is effective before purchasing or making it.

You will need to treat your Corgi monthly. Create a reminder on your phone or other device so that you do not miss one of the treatments.

Worms and Parasites

While worms and other less common parasites aren't likely to be a problem, you still want to make sure there is virtually no chance that your Corgi will contract them. There are many types of worms that could become a problem:

- Heartworms
- Hookworms
- Roundworms
- Tapeworms
- Whipworms

Many of the signs of these parasites are difficult to identify, at least in the early stages. If your dog exhibits any of the following signs, make an appointment with your vet to have your dog checked for one of the different, less common parasites.

- Your Corgi is unexpectedly lethargic.
- Patches of fur begin to fall out (this will be noticeably if you brush your Corgi regularly) or if you notice patchy spaces in your dog's coat.
- Your Corgi's stomach becomes distended (expands and looks like a potbelly). If this happens, set up an appointment immediately to have it checked.
- Your dog begins coughing, vomiting, has diarrhea, or has a loss in appetite.

Any of these symptoms can be incredibly telling in this high-energy breed, so set up an appointment as soon as you notice any of these changes to remove the problem and get your Corgi back to the healthy canine you want it to be.

If your vet diagnoses your Corgi with either hookworms or roundworms, you will need to set up an appointment with your doctor for yourself. Both of these worms can be contracted through skin contact, so if your dog has one of them, it is highly likely that you do as well. You will need to be treated to ensure that you do not suffer, and that you and your dog do not continue to perpetuate them in your home.

Heartworms are something you should be actively trying to prevent because they are a potentially deadly parasite. There are medicines that will ensure your dog does not contract them.

Benefits of Veterinarians

You should visit the vet annually for checkups and shots. Just as people have annual visits, dogs need to be seen on a regular basis.

Because it is a high-energy dog, it is likely you will notice if there is a potential problem with your Corgi, but it is not guaranteed. Annual visits will make sure there isn't something that is slow-acting draining your dog. Corgis are also less likely than some dogs to show when they are injured. A vet can identify when a Corgi is doing too much or has an injury that the Corgi simply hasn't noticed. After all, if your Corgi knows that injuries mean fewer adventures and walks, it is likely to hide or ignore an injury rather than miss out on the chance to spend time with you.

Health checkups are also good to make sure that your dog is aging well. If there are any early symptoms of something wrong with your dog as it ages (such as arthritis), you will be able to start making adjustments for it. The vet can help you come up with new ways to manage your Corgi's health so that you don't have to reduce the amount of time you spend together. You may need to start taking shorter, more frequent walks, spend a little more time playing at home, or hike on easier paths. In the end it is worth it to be able to keep your Corgi going strong for as long as possible.

Holistic Alternatives

It is understandable that so many people are seeking a more holistic approach to taking care of their pets. However, you have to spend a good bit of time researching to make sure you are not taking unnecessary risks. Unverified holistic medicines can be a waste of time and money at best, and potentially dangerous at their worst.

If you would like to use a holistic medication on your Corgi, ask for your vet's opinion, and check with several other Corgi experts to see what the consensus is before you start. Conduct your own online research on neutral sites. Read what scientists have said about the medicine. There is a chance that the products you buy from a store are actually better than some of the medications sold as holistic.

Make sure you are thorough and that you do not take any unnecessary risks with your Corgi.

Photo Courtesy of
Sunny Hanford

Vaccinating Your Corgi

Corgis have the same vaccination schedule as most other breeds.

The first shots are required between six and eight weeks following the Corgi's birth. You should find out from the breeder if these have been taken care of and get the records of the shots:

- Corona virus
- Distemper
- Hepatitis
- Leptospirosis
- Parainfluenza
- Parvo
- These same shots are required again at between ten and twelve weeks of age.
- These same shots are required again along with the first rabies shot between fourteen and fifteen weeks of age.
- You dog will need to get these shots (including the rabies shot) annually after that.

If you actually plan to use your Corgi as a farm dog or for other strenuous work, it will need other shots. Consult with your vet to see what else your Corgi will need based on the kind of work it will be doing. Make sure to get the schedule for upkeep on these shots.

CHAPTER 17

Health Concerns

All pure-bred dogs, including Corgis, have illnesses and genetic problems that you have to monitor your dog for. Regardless of how you found your furry family member, you can monitor your Corgi for signs and symptoms related to the genetic illnesses that are common in Corgis. If your dog starts to show signs or symptoms of one of these illnesses, set up an appointment with your vet to have your Corgi checked out.

If you start with a puppy, there are a lot of things you can do to ensure the health of your dog. The breeder should have health records for the shots and required testing. All of the details on the genetic and common ailments of Corgis are in Chapter 4. Knowing about the health of its parents is one of the best ways of knowing how healthy your Corgi will be, but no breed is perfect or free of problems, no matter how healthy

Photo Courtesy of
Jennifer Durward

the parents are. If your Corgi's parents came from a line where some of these illnesses were present, there is a chance that your dog will also have these problems, even if its parents did not. You should be aware of these issues so that you can keep an eye on your Corgi as it ages.

Corgis are a relatively healthy breed, especially for one with such a long history.

Where You Can Go Wrong

Any thoroughbred canine needs to be tested for genetic problems because that lets you know what you should watch for and what you can do if your dog starts to present the genetic problems. You should always be aware of these potential problems so that you can take better care of your Corgi.

Diet

Probably the easiest thing you can do for your Corgi, though, is to make sure that it always has a healthy, well-balanced diet and plenty of exercise. Because of their small stature, Corgis cannot handle a lot of extra weight on their bodies.

Just because your Corgi is gaining weight does not mean that the problem is food related. Hypothyroidism is another issue that could cause your dog to gain weight. If your Corgi is gaining weight and you are certain that it isn't food related, you should take your dog to the vet to see if this is the problem. Lethargy is another indication of hypothyroidism.

If you ensure your dog gets a healthy diet (with only the rare exception or treat), it will be easier to determine if hypothyroidism is the problem, and not excessive food intake.

Exercise

Corgis love to move around, which you may forget since they also love just being with you. If you prefer a sedentary lifestyle, a Corgi is not a good dog for you. They require several walks a day (or a couple of very long walks). They will not require as much activity as the larger working dogs (especially dogs like Huskies, Dalmatians, and Blue Heelers), but they still require more exercise than almost any other dog their size. Corgis may be a short breed, but they are packed full of energy.

If your Corgi is destructive after the puppy years, it probably means that you are not exercising it enough. Make more time to go out and walk, participate in Corgi-related events, go to dog parks, or go hiking. Your Corgi will be much happier for it, and you will lose fewer things to destructive boredom.

However, the most important reason to exercise your Corgi enough is that a sedentary Corgi is very likely to gain weight, a problem that their frames really cannot handle.

Importance of the Breeder to Ensuring Health in Your Corgi

Because Corgis have such a long history, there is a lot that breeders should already know about taking care of their puppies the right way. This includes testing. If you work with a breeder who is part of one of the Corgi organizations (whether Pembroke or Cardigan), they are required to be honest and up-front about potential health issues. The history of the breed is well documented, so no genetic diseases should be a surprise to new Corgi parents.

If the breeder cannot provide you with a health guarantee about your Corgi puppy, do not purchase a puppy from that breeder. If a breeder says that a puppy or litter has to be kept in an isolated location for health reasons, do not work with that breeder.

Ask the breeder to talk about the history of the parents, the kinds of health problems that have been in the family, and if the breeder has had problems with any particular illness in the past. If the breeder gives you only short or vague answers, this is a sign that you may be getting a Corgi that will have serious health problems later.

Also work with a breeder who takes the time to talk about the health issues and problems, can give you a detailed history of the parents and previous litters, and is willing to answer your questions.

Common Diseases and Conditions

Corgis do have a few common ailments that you should know about before you bring your puppy home:

- Hip dysplasia
- Retinal dysplasia and pupillary membranes
- Progressive retinal atrophy (PRA)
- Hypothyroidism
- Cryptorchidism
- Epilepsy
- Reproductive issues

- Degenerative myelopathy (testing will help detect this debilitating and incurable genetic problem)
- Intervertebral disc disease (IVDD), which is associated with their long backs
- Willebrand's Disease (a blood clotting health problem)

Cardigans may also have the following ailments:

- Cataracts, glaucoma, lens luxation, and eyelash abnormalities
- Allergies
- Immunoglobulin deficiency (a rare but serious immune system disorder)

Photo Courtesy of
Elizabeth Schiavello

Many of these conditions should be tested for before you bring your puppy home. If you bring home an older dog and cannot get health records for your new family member, you can take it to the vet for testing. Regular visits to the vet will help you detect any non-genetic disorders, like problems stemming from their long backs. Your vet can also let you know when you are over-feeding your dog, or when weight is becoming a concern (since it is often hard to see these kinds of problems on your own).

Prevention & Monitoring

Apart from genetic issues (which you should learn about from the breeder and the vet history of the puppy), the biggest problem Corgis face is obesity. They love to eat and are clever enough to find ways to get to food that you would not ever consider. Making sure it cannot access your food is one of the best things you can do for your Corgi. Taking it out for regular strenuous (or frequent) exercise is another.

Do monitor your Corgi for other potential problems as your dog is not likely to let them get in the way of having fun. Watch your Corgi for signs of IVDD, a condition that means one of your canine's spinal discs has either ruptured or it is bulging. Ask your vet for the signs that this could be a problem (it is common in all short dogs with long backs). If your Corgi shows any sign of a disc problem, immediately take it to the vet. Often crate rest and light medication will fix early signs. However, if it is more serious surgery may be required.

*Photo Courtesy of
Susan Dale*

CHAPTER 18

Your Aging Corgi

Corgis have an average life span of between eleven and thirteen years, giving you more than a decade with your amazing companion. By the age of nine years, your Corgi is a senior canine. As your Corgi ages, you will need to start making adjustments to help it age without having to give up so many of the things that the two of you love doing together. Many of these adjustments will need to be made based on each individual Corgi's abilities. Your dog may age slowly at first, and then suddenly start showing its age within a few weeks. You will need to know your dog's changing limits so that you can continue to be active without pushing your dog too far.

Photo Courtesy of Betsy Ellsworth

Corgis may slow down, but they don't tend to be curmudgeons like many of the other small to medium dog breeds. They are still peppy and friendly well into their golden years, making it easy to forget that they simply are not capable of doing the things they once did. That means that you can enjoy the later years just as much as the early ones, except you won't have to dedicate nearly so much time to training and behavior issues. Instead you will be able to relax and enjoy a calmer life. It is easy to make the senior years incredibly enjoyable for your Corgi by making the necessary adjustments that allow your dog to keep being active without overexertion.

Senior Dog Care

Photo Courtesy of Sunny Hanford

Your Corgi is going to be far easier to care for as a senior than at any other point in its life. Naps will be just as exciting as walks. Sleeping beside you while you watch something or even napping with you is pretty much all it takes to make your Corgi happy.

However, you must continue to be vigilant about diet and exercise. Now is not the time to let your Corgi start to eat anything and everything or neglect to take your regular walks. A senior Corgi cannot handle extra weight, so you must be careful to ensure it remains healthy even as it ages.

If your canine cannot manage long walks anymore, make the walks shorter and more numerous and spend more time romping around your yard or home.

When it comes to items that your Corgi will need to access regularly, you will need to make some changes to your current configuration.

- Set water bowls out in a couple of different places so that your dog can easily reach them as needed. If your Corgi has issues with its spine, you can place slightly raised water dishes around the home to make drinking easier.

- Cover hard floor surfaces (such as tiles, hardwood, and vinyl). Use carpets or rugs that will not slip out from under your Corgi.

- Add cushions and softer bedding where your Corgi sleeps. This will both make the surface more comfortable and help your Corgi stay warmer. There are some bed warmers for dogs if your Corgi displays achy joints or muscles often.

- Increase how often you brush your Corgi to improve its circulation. This should be very agreeable to your Corgi as a way to make up for other limitations on your activities together.

- Stay inside in extreme heat and cold. Your Corgi is hardy, but its old canine body cannot handle the extreme changes as well as once it did.

- Use stairs or ramps for your Corgi instead of constantly picking up your canine. Picking your Corgi up may be more convenient, but it is not healthy for either of you. Let your dog maintain a bit more self-sufficiency.

- Avoid changing your furniture around, particularly if your Corgi shows signs of having trouble with its vision. A familiar home is more comforting and less stressful. If your Corgi is not able to see as clearly, keeping the home familiar will make it easier for your dog to move around without getting hurt.

- If you have stairs, consider setting up an area where your dog can stay without having to use the stairs as often.

- Create a space where your Corgi can relax with fewer distractions and noises. Your Corgi probably will not want to be alone often, but you should have a place where you and your older dog can just relax without loud or startling noises.

- Be prepared to let your dog out more often for restroom breaks.

Nutrition

Since a decrease in exercise is inevitable for aging Corgis, you will need to adjust the diet. If you opt to feed your Corgi commercial dog food, make sure you change to the senior food. If you make your Corgi's food, take the time to research how best to reduce calories without sacrificing taste. Your canine is going to need less fat in its food, so you may need to find something healthier that still tastes good to supplement the types of foods you gave your Corgi as a puppy or an active adult dog.

Exercise

Exercise will be a bit trickier because your Corgi is not going to want to admit that the kinds of activities you used to do are just too difficult now. It is up to you to adjust the schedule and keep your Corgi happily active. Usually increasing the number of walks while decreasing the duration will help keep your Corgi as active as necessary.

Keep in mind that your Corgi is more likely to gain weight in the later years, something that its body really cannot handle. Make sure that activity is not reduced too much so that your canine does not become obese.

This will probably be the hardest part of watching your Corgi age. However, you will need to watch your Corgi for signs of tiredness or pain so that you can stop exercising before your dog has done too much. Your pace will need to be slower and your attention more on your dog, but ultimately it can be just as rewarding. You will probably notice that your Corgi spends more time sniffing. This could be a sign that your dog is tiring, or it could be your dog's way of acknowledging that long steady walks are a thing of the past and it is ready to stop to enjoy the little things more. It is an interesting time and gives you a chance to get to understand your Corgi as the years start to show.

Mental Stimulation

Unlike its body, your Corgi's mind is likely going to be just as sharp and clever in the golden years. That means you can start making adjustments to focus more on activities that are mentally stimulating. You can start doing training for fun because your Corgi will be just as able to learn now as when it was one year old. Actually, it is likely to be easier as your Corgi has learned to focus better.

Your Corgi will be grateful for the shift in focus and additional attention. Getting your senior Corgi new toys is one way to help keep your dog's mind active if you do not want to spend time training. You can then teach the Corgi different names for the toys because that is something that will interest your Corgi (after all, it will still work for praise). Whatever toys you get, make sure they are not too rough on your dog's older jaws and teeth.

Hide and seek is another game that your aging Corgi can manage with relative ease. Whether you hide toys or yourself, this can be a game that keeps your Corgi guessing.

Regular Vet Exams

Just as humans go to doctors more often as they age, your Corgi is going to need to visit the vet with greater frequency. The vet can make sure that your Corgi is staying active without being too active, and that there is no unnecessary stress on your older dog. If your canine has sustained an injury and hidden it from you, your vet is more likely to detect it.

Your vet can also make recommendations about activities and changes to your schedule based on your Corgi's physical abilities and any changes in personality. For example, if your Corgi is panting more now, it could be a sign of pain from stiffness. Your vet can help you determine the best way to keep your Corgi happy and active during the later years.

Common Old-age Aliments

Chapter 17 covers the illnesses that are common or likely with Corgis, but old age tends to bring a slew of ailments that are not particular to any one breed. Here are the things you will need to watch for (as well as talking to your vet about them).

- Diabetes is probably the greatest concern for a breed that loves to eat as much as Corgis do, especially with their small frame. Though it is usually thought of as a genetic condition, any Corgi can become diabetic if not fed and exercised properly. This is another reason why it is so important to be careful with your Corgi's diet and exercise levels.

- Arthritis is probably the most common ailment in any breed, and Corgis are no exception. If your dog is showing signs of stiffness and pain after normal activities, it is very likely that it has arthritis. Talk with your vet about safe ways to help minimize the pain and discomfort of this common joint ailment.

- Gum disease is a common issue in older dogs as well, and you should be just as vigilant about brushing teeth when your dog gets older as you are at any other age. A regular check on your Corgi's teeth and gums can help ensure this is not a problem.

- Loss of eyesight or blindness is relatively common in older dogs, just as it is in humans. Unlike humans, however, dogs don't do well with glasses. Have your dog's vision checked at least once a year, and more often if it is obvious that its eyesight is failing.

- Kidney disease is a common problem in older dogs, and one that you should monitor for the older your Corgi gets. If your canine is drinking more often and having accidents regularly, this could be a sign of something more serious than just aging. If you notice this happening, get your Corgi to the vet as soon as possible and have it checked for kidney disease.

Enjoying the Final Years

The last years of your Corgi's life can actually be just as enjoyable (if not more so) than earlier stages. The energy and activities that you used to do will be replaced with more attention and relaxation than at any other time. Finally having your Corgi be calm enough to just sit still and enjoy your company can be incredibly nice (just remember to keep up its

Photo Courtesy of Elizabeth Schiavello

activity levels instead of getting too complacent with your Corgi's new-found love of resting and relaxing).

Steps and Ramps

Corgis are small, but that does not mean that you should be picking them up more often as they age. There are two good reasons to ensure your Corgi your Corgi is able to move around without being picked up.

- Their long spines mean it is less safe and healthy to be picked up often.
- Independence in movement is best for you and your Corgi. You do not want your Corgi to come to expect to be picked up every time it wants to get on the furniture or into the car.

Steps and ramps are the best way to ensure your Corgi is not too pampered (perhaps spoiled is a better word). It also keeps your dog's back from unnecessary stress.

Enjoy the Advantages

Corgis can be a lot of fun in their old age. They are still smart as can be, but they have learned to chill a bit more. Their personality will change a little, but usually it just means they are more likely to want to relax with you.

They make fantastic therapy dogs, so you can take them to places where therapy dogs are needed (particularly nursing homes). This can be a great way to relax or release frustration after a long or difficult day. Older Corgis are a fantastic companion to come home to because they want nothing more than to be with you. As long as you are there, they are happy. Sometimes that is all it takes to turn a disaster of a day into something bearable.

They will find the warmest and most comfortable places, and they will want you to join them.

They are incredibly devoted and will be happy to just share a short stroll followed by a lazy evening at home.

What to Expect from an Older Pembroke

Older Pembrokes are just as friendly as they ever were, they just have limitations they are not accustomed to. Help your Pembroke adjust to the limitations and make sure it knows that you are there just as much as before so that it feels less stress. Your happiness is still of utmost importance, so make sure you let your Pembroke know that you feel the same way about it that you always have. Inclusion is incredibly important.

What to Expect from an Older Cardigan

Cardigans are more likely to display grumpy behavior and are more inclined to being lazy if you don't keep them exercising. Since they are more inclined to be relaxed over the course of their lives, the transition will not be nearly as difficult. You may need to give them a place of their own if you have company, though, because they may not handle extra noise as well as their Pembroke counterparts.

Photo Courtesy of Elizabeth Schiavello